CHRONICLES OF THE BIBLE

From Creation to Eternity

Chronicles of the Bible
© 2025 Isaac J. Young

This is a work of narrative retelling. While based on biblical texts and historical traditions, it is presented in a format to inspire, educate, and engage readers. Any departures from direct translation are for the sake of storytelling.

ISBN 979-8-90046-473-2

Table of Contents

Prologue

There is a story older than nations and older than empires. It is a story of people who stumble, hope, rebel, and cry out, sometimes receiving answers in mysterious ways. It is the story of covenant, exile and return, of prophets, kings, and visionaries trying to speak God's words into the chaos of human life.

The Bible is not a single tale in one voice. It is a chorus of songs, laws, histories, letters, and visions and sometimes poetic, sometimes practical, full of joy and grief. Across every page runs a single thread, God is at work, and nothing is beyond hope.

The "Chronicles of the Bible" brings this vast story to life in an accessible and engaging way, showing the full sweep of the narrative so you can see the people, events, and promises in one concise and flowing account.

Chapter One - Creation of the world

In the beginning, there was nothing, or at least, nothing like anything we recognise today. No mountains, no seas, no sun, no moon, no birds in the sky or fish in the water. The cosmos was an empty, dark expanse, and yet, somehow, it was pregnant with possibility. Into this void, God spoke, and the universe, quite literally, began to listen.

First came light, splitting the dark with a boldness that would become a recurring theme in the story of creation, light against darkness, life against emptiness, order against chaos. Day one was light, night followed, and a rhythm began, a heartbeat for the world.

Then came the sky, the waters above and below drawn apart as if the universe itself were stretching and yawning. Land emerged from the water, fields and forests and deserts taking shape, a patchwork quilt of terrain, waiting for life to make its mark. Vegetation followed with grasses, trees, and flowers all producing seeds so life could perpetuate itself without human interference. It was a world designed to flourish, resilient and self-renewing.

The sun, moon, and stars were placed next, to govern the cycles of day and night, seasons, and years, a cosmic clock for the rhythm of life to come. Birds took to the sky, fish to the seas, and all living creatures filled the lands and waters in a riot of movement and colour. The world was teeming, bustling, abundant beyond imagination.

And then humanity came. Made in God's image, humans were not just part of creation they were its stewards, entrusted with tending, naming, and caring for the world. Adam and Eve were made from flesh and blood yet echoing the divine, a spark of intelligence, creativity, and curiosity that set them apart from the rest of creation.

This was a world full of promise. It was a world of order, beauty, and rhythm, designed to sustain life and reflect the character of its Maker. Yet even in this perfection, there was space for choice, for responsibility, and, inevitably, for the beginnings of struggle.

Creation was not just an event in the past. It was a stage set, a prelude to the entire human story. It was the opening act in the grand narrative of the Bible, where light confronts darkness, life confronts emptiness, and God's voice begins to weave a story that would stretch from the first breath to the promise of a new heaven and new earth.

And so the world began, full of possibility, brimming with potential, and waiting for the human story to unfold.

Chapter Two - The Garden and the First Humans

So here we are. The stage has been set. Light fills the sky. Seas have settled reluctantly into their appointed places. Mountains and valleys argue quietly over whose peaks get the best sunrise. Rivers wander aimlessly but loyally to the oceans, and life, oh life is everywhere, busy and insistent. And then, at last, the crown of creation enters: humans.

They are Adam and Eve, though the Bible's retelling, when revisited with a modern eye, lets us pause and imagine them in more detail than a single sentence allows. Picture Adam, the first man, opening his eyes for the first time and blinking at a world so vividly alive it might make a modern tourist gasp. He is tall, untested, untroubled by worries, and probably very confused. He stands in a garden so lush it could have been designed by a committee of angels who took their roles as decorators far too seriously. Fruit-laden trees lean toward one another in conspiratorial clusters, rivers sparkle as though they have just discovered themselves and every animal nearby seems to be quietly judging him with innocent curiosity.

Eve comes next, fashioned with care, thoughtfulness, and perhaps just a dash of theatrical flair. She is Adam's companion, equal in intellect and wonder, capable of thought, observation, and laughter. Together, they wander the garden with an open-ended curiosity, naming creatures, touching leaves, loving the colours, the scents, the way the breeze whispers through the trees. They are, at first, utterly at home in this paradise.

And yet, paradise is always a delicate thing. The garden is full of abundance and beauty, but it is not unlimited. There is one rule, a single instruction, apparently simple but fraught with significance: do not eat from the tree in the middle of the garden, the one the Bible calls the tree of the knowledge of good and evil. It sits there, leaves shimmering, fruit gleaming, quite possibly tempting just by existing. And, if we are honest, temptation has never required much more than a little gleam.

Adam and Eve might have wandered past it, lightly, almost absentmindedly. But of course, it would have caught their eye. Imagine standing before something that is simultaneously beautiful and forbidden. Curiosity, a peculiarly human trait, stirs. *Surely a little nibble couldn't hurt...* And so the first act of hesitation, the first taste of moral choice, enters human history.

Enter the serpent, slithering through the narrative like a mischievous stagehand, quietly whispering possibilities. The serpent doesn't shout, it doesn't demand, it simply suggests. And suggestion is often stronger than command. "You won't die," it hisses, in tones that could charm a hawk from the sky.

"Surely you will be like the divine, knowing good and evil, seeing as the gods do." It's persuasive, subtle, infinitely patient, and it knows humans far better than humans know themselves.

Eve, curious and thoughtful, listens. She regards the fruit, turns it over in her hands, smells it, perhaps even admires the way the light catches its skin. She bites. And then, for reasons that will forever fascinate theologians, historians, and psychologists alike, she offers it to Adam, who eats it too. Just like that, the first humans act with agency, choosing knowledge over innocence, curiosity over obedience. And the world shifts.

Immediately, they notice the change. Awareness blooms in their minds like fire suddenly kindled. Suddenly, they understand more than they had known before. The garden, once a place of simple joy, now feels layered with complexity. They see the difference between right and wrong, feel fear for the first time, and discover a profound and peculiar sense of shame. They fashion clothes, primitive though they are from leaves, an early human solution to an entirely new problem.

God, when He walks into the garden to check on them, does not merely scold. There is a mix of disappointment and inevitability. Creation, after all, is a theatre of free will as much as it is a masterpiece of design. The humans, having exercised choice, must now experience consequence. They are exiled. The garden, with its rivers and fruit and innocence, is closed to them, and they are sent out into the wider world, a world that will now be far more complicated, more challenging, more demanding.

And what a world it is. Outside the garden, life is still beautiful but unpredictable. Animals are no longer entirely companions. Some are predators, some are wary of humans, some indifferent. The ground is fertile but requires effort to work. Food is still available but no longer delivered on demand. The first humans learn, in their very first days of exile, the strange balance of beauty and struggle, wonder and difficulty. They carry with them knowledge, curiosity, and the seeds of all human history and important traits like innovation, courage, fallibility, and imagination.

It is striking how vividly this story captures both the grandeur and the absurdity of being human. We begin in a place of unimaginable beauty, with every need provided and every curiosity ready to explore. And yet, we leave it, propelled by curiosity and choice, stepping into a world where everything must be earned and understood. Eden is not lost forever but rather it persists in memory, in myth, in longing. But humanity's story, from this moment onward, is one of journey, discovery, and, inevitably, redemption.

The first humans are out in the world, feet on the ground, eyes open, hearts learning courage, and minds ever aware of possibility. The garden, lush and perfect, remains in the background being a reminder of beginnings, of innocence, and of a world that waits, always, to be understood, explored, and cherished.

Chapter Three - Life in Exile

Adam and Eve found that the world now greeted them with the kind of raw honesty that only reality can muster. Eden had been... well, Eden. Soft light, soft fruit, rivers that did what rivers are supposed to do without complaint. Outside its borders, however, life was not quite so obliging. Nature, which had been kindly and ornamental inside the garden, now revealed itself as capricious, sometimes threatening, and endlessly surprising.

The first thing the humans noticed was the sheer size of everything. Mountains were taller than they could easily climb. Trees seemed impossibly vast, their roots tangled like the hair of an untamed giant. Rivers roared or meandered unpredictably. They were no longer tidy garden streams but rivers with moods, sometimes gentle, sometimes violent, and always in a hurry. The sun was harsher here, the rain wetter, the nights colder. Eden had been a friendly tutor. The wider world was more like a professor who delighted in tricky examinations.

They had to learn quickly. Before, food had been handed to them in abundance, now they needed to search, to forage, to understand. They discovered which fruits were safe and which carried hidden dangers, an experiment repeated countless times with varying degrees of success. Some leaves, once thought edible, caused surprise reactions, including mild discomfort, sudden sneezes, stomach groans, and, in one memorable instance, a rash that lasted a few days. It was education in a rather literal, corporeal way.

Animals, too, demanded attention. In Eden, they had been companions, perhaps even curious onlookers, but out here, the balance had shifted. Some animals were indifferent, some wary, and some, as Adam quickly discovered, were decidedly predatory. Eve noted the alertness of birds, the sudden swish of tails in the underbrush, the gleam in eyes. Learning to observe, to anticipate, to respect, became a daily necessity. Survival required more than strength. It required attention, patience, and, most of all, humility.

Yet there was joy too. Humans had a peculiar capacity to notice beauty even in difficulty. They could marvel at a sunrise splitting a valley, at dew sparkling on a leaf, at the curious dance of insects. Each day, as they foraged and explored, they found not only sustenance but fascination. Adam was endlessly intrigued by rocks, their varied textures and colours. Eve delighted in the wind, the way it rustled grass and leaves, carrying scents from places they had not yet visited. Even in a world more challenging than Eden, wonder persisted.

Sleep, too, became a subject of discovery. In Eden, there had been a sense of ease, a rhythm without effort. Now, humans had to find safe places to rest. Adam experimented with lying beneath trees, on soft moss, and, once, in a shallow cave, discovering that some locations were warmer, quieter, or simply less likely to provoke curious animals. Eve observed the stars and learned their patterns, noting which constellations rose first, which indicated approaching storms. In this way, nights became lessons, as much about the world as about themselves.

Over time, the humans began to notice subtle patterns in the land. Certain berries grew near particular stones. Rivers overflowed predictably after heavy rains. Birds migrated. Predators followed trails of water and prey. Slowly, Adam and Eve began to map, to plan, to organise their survival. They learned to store food in rudimentary ways, to move cautiously through forests, to signal each other when danger approached. Civilization, in its earliest form, was taking root, not in cities, not in governments, but in attention, knowledge, and cooperation.

They also discovered companionship in new ways. Beyond mere survival, conversation became essential. Words were tools as important as hands or eyes. Eve described what she saw, Adam pointed out what he had learned. Together, they shared observations, invented names for things, argued over strategies for finding water or shelter, and laughed at small disasters, the sudden collapse of a precarious berry stack, a slip on wet stone, and an awkward encounter with a particularly bold bird. Language, they realised, was more than communication. It was a bridge between curiosity and understanding, between wonder and action.

And then there was play, a strange and wonderful human tendency. Amidst danger and work, humans instinctively create diversion. Adam discovered that rolling down gentle slopes was thrilling. Eve found joy in tossing pebbles into streams, observing ripples, counting skips across water. Animals became participants in these games, sometimes willingly, sometimes as uncooperative observers. These moments, small as they seemed, were vital. These were the first hints that humans could enjoy life even when it was difficult, that curiosity and creativity were as essential to survival as food or shelter.

Time passed. The first humans learned the rhythms of the land, which plants flowered first, which animals came with the seasons, which nights brought frost or fog. They discovered the importance of observation, of memory, of planning. Every day was a lesson. Every night, reflection. And slowly, almost imperceptibly, they began to shape the world around them, not with tools of iron or stone (that would come later) but with attention, care, and understanding.

Eden may have been behind them, but the garden's lessons lingered. The abundance they once took for granted had taught them to appreciate nourishment, the innocence of discovery had shown them the joy of curiosity, and the simplicity of paradise had underscored the value of cooperation. Life outside Eden was harder, yes, but it was no less beautiful. Perhaps, in some ways, it was even more vivid, because now they were participants in a world that responded, that challenged, that demanded engagement and courage.

And so the early world beyond Eden unfolded, day by day, observation by observation, step by cautious step. Adam and Eve were explorers, learners, and, in their own imperfect way, pioneers. They faced challenges they had never imagined, discovered resources they had never noticed, and began the slow, staggering, wondrous task of becoming human in the fullest sense, extremely curious, capable, resilient, and endlessly fascinated by the world they now called home.

Chapter Four - Cain, Abel, and the First Steps of Humanity

If Eden was the garden stage set for innocence, what comes next is the sobering curtain rise on what it actually means to be human. For Adam and Eve, life after exile was not simply an inconvenience, like moving from a palace to a modest cottage. It was an entirely new existence, harder, rawer, and tinged with a sense that something once effortless was now forever out of reach. Still, life continued. And with it came children.

The firstborn was Cain. His very name carried the suggestion of possession. Eve held him up like a small miracle, which of course he was. Not long after came Abel, whose name, by contrast, meant something closer to breath or vapour, a fleeting exhalation that suggested fragility. The irony would prove almost prophetic.

Cain and Abel grew into young men, each carving out a role in this newly minted world. Cain was a tiller of the soil, coaxing food from reluctant earth. Abel was a shepherd, guiding his flocks across fields that had never known a fence or a marketplace. They were, in a way, humanity's first experiment in specialisation. It wasn't long before each decided to bring an offering to God, Cain from his crops, Abel from his flocks.

Here the story takes a turn that theologians and scholars have wrangled over for millennia. Abel's offering, fat portions from the firstborn of his sheep, found favour with God. Cain's offering of grain and produce did not. Why? Was it the quality? The spirit behind the gift? Or perhaps the larger point is that life, even in its earliest chapters, is not always fair or symmetrical. Some things are accepted, some are not, and we are left to wrestle with the difference.

Cain certainly did. He smouldered. Anger seeped into him like dye in cloth. God warns him, almost like a kindly parent trying to explain consequences to a stubborn child: "Sin is crouching at your door and it desires to have you, but you must rule over it." But Cain, it seems, was not listening. Or perhaps he listened and decided otherwise.

One day, out in the fields where Abel tended his flocks, Cain acted. He invited his brother, perhaps with a calm voice, and then struck him down. Just like that, humanity's first murder, the first spilling of blood by human hand, stained the earth. Abel, whose name already suggested a passing breath, was gone in a moment.

It is hard to overstate the gravity of this scene. Until now, the world had known disobedience, labour, exile, even shame, but not yet the taking of human life by another human life. Here, at the very dawn of human history, jealousy and anger erupted into violence. It is a story that has echoed through centuries, replayed in countless variations, a sobering reminder that civilisation's oldest sibling rivalry was also its first crime.

When God asked Cain where Abel was, Cain responded with the infamous deflection: "Am I my brother's keeper?" It was, if you think about it, both a question and an answer. It was a refusal to accept responsibility and a declaration of detachment. And yet the irony is that the story itself insists the opposite. Yes, you are your brother's keeper. Always have been, always will be.

But the deed could not be undone. Abel's blood cried out from the ground. And Cain, the first murderer, became also the first wanderer. He was marked but not killed, not erased, but given a strange kind of protection that ensured his survival even as he moved restlessly across the earth. It was a punishment and a mercy woven together, a paradox as old as humanity itself.

From there, we pivot to early humanity in general. Cain built a city, which is remarkable if you think about it, one man, marked as a restless wanderer, also becomes the father of urban life. His descendants forged tools, created music, invented the arts of living. Violence entered the story, but so too did culture. This was messy from the start, but it was undeniably fertile.

As generations unfolded, humanity multiplied. Some lived in tents, some worked with bronze and iron, some plucked strings and beat drums, all finding ways to carve meaning out of existence. We won't linger on technical detail, whether they used stone hammers or how they learned to kindle fire, but we can focus on one thing. Humanity, even in its brokenness, kept moving forward. The world grew noisier, busier, more complicated.

And beneath it all, a quiet pattern began to form. Wherever humans went, so too went creativity and corruption, brilliance and brutality. Abel's breath was short, Cain's mark was long, and together they set the tone for everything to come.

Generations continued to unfold like ripples from a stone tossed in a pond. Cain's descendants experimented. They invented tents, which made life less soggy in the rain. They raised livestock not only for food but for milk and hides. Music arrived, seemingly out of nowhere, as one descendant discovered the peculiar joy of plucking a string stretched across a bow or striking a hollowed-out log. Before long there were lyres, flutes, rhythms, and melodies. Another descendant, Tubal-Cain, hammered bronze and iron into tools, weapons, and ornaments, ushering in what we would now grandly call the age of metallurgy.

So, in quick succession, humanity had architecture, agriculture, music, metallurgy. Not bad for a few generations. It was as if, once expelled from Eden, humans were determined to make up for it by reshaping the world in their own image. They could no longer stroll through a perfect garden, so they built shelters. They could no longer rely on fruit dropping into their hands, so they tilled fields and bred animals. They could no longer hear the unfiltered voice of God walking in the cool of the day, so they filled the air with the sound of drums and pipes.

But alongside invention came something darker. Violence began to fester. Lamech, a descendant of Cain, boasts of killing a man for wounding him, even composing a little song about it. If Cain's act had been an isolated tragedy, Lamech turned it into swagger. Violence was no longer an exception but an emerging rhythm of its own.

Meanwhile, Adam and Eve had other children, and from their line came Seth, born as something of a fresh start after Abel's death. Seth's descendants, too, multiplied, and with them also a flicker of hope "At that time people began to call on the name of the Lord." In other words, worship, prayer, some form of seeking, entered the story. Humanity was not only building and killing, it was also reaching upward.

What follows is one of those great genealogical stretches, which in its own way is astonishing. The lifespans are epic, hundreds of years, entire centuries strung together like pearls on a cord. Each name marks another link in the chain, another reminder that life did not flicker out but surged forward with stubborn momentum. Among them, one stands out: Enoch, who "walked with God" so closely that he did not taste death in the usual way but was simply taken. It is a small but luminous exception in an otherwise steady roll call of births and deaths, a hint that intimacy with God was still possible, even in a bruised and broken world.

And yet, the overall trend is sobering. As humanity spread across the earth, so too did corruption. Violence, greed, arrogance, these grew alongside culture and innovation, like weeds that refuse to be separated from the wheat. The world was becoming crowded not just with people but with their choices, their conflicts, and their appetites.

By the time we near the story of Noah, the tone shifts palpably, the world tilting dangerously off balance. The earth was full of violence and imaginations were increasingly bent toward evil. Humanity, it seemed, had taken its first great leap forward, and its first great lurch sideways. Progress and decay marched arm in arm, inseparable companions.

Something ominous gathers on the horizon. The Creator who once looked upon all that was made and called it "good" now looks again, and the verdict is heavier, more sorrowful.

Humanity has walked far from Eden, and though the garden gate is long behind them, the echo of its loss still lingers. What began with creation and innocence has become a tale of brilliance and blood, of cities and songs, of violence and hope. The world is alive with people now, but not all is well.

Chapter Five - The flood and Noah

Noah arrives on the scene, humanity has grown inventive, populous, and profoundly unruly. The genealogies unspool like a family tree gone feral, names branching out into clans, clans spreading into territories, and with each generation the sheer busyness of human life intensifies. But alongside the music and metallurgy, alongside tents and cities and the chatter of children's voices, there was also something darker. The earth had become corrupt and full of violence. It is as though everything had spun off course.

Imagine, if you will, God surveying the world like a disappointed gardener. At creation's dawn, everything had been fresh, green, teeming with promise. Now the weeds had taken over, the soil was exhausted, and the garden path was clogged with brambles. Humanity had not simply stumbled. It had cultivated wickedness with alarming success.

Enter Noah, a man described as "righteous in his generation." Which, if you think about it, is a backhanded sort of compliment. Being righteous in a thoroughly corrupt world is rather like being the only person at a festival who remembers to shower. You stand out. And Noah did. While others schemed and swaggered, he walked with God. It was enough to catch heaven's attention.

And so came the plan. Not a tweak, not a correction, but a reset of large proportions. A flood, vast enough to scrub the world clean, leaving only a remnant to begin again. It is a terrifying notion, and yet it is presented with matter-of-factness, as though announcing a particularly heavy rain was on the way.

Noah was given instructions, detailed ones, at that. Build an ark, he was told, three hundred cubits long, fifty wide, thirty high. For those of us less comfortable with cubits, that's something like a football pitch and a half in length, as tall as a modest apartment block, and broad enough to house almost anything you can imagine. It wasn't a boat so much as a floating warehouse. To build such a thing in the ancient world must have seemed laughably absurd. Neighbours surely gathered, shaking their heads, muttering about old Noah and his folly. But Noah set to work anyway, hammering and hewing, fashioning gopher wood into beams, smearing pitch across planks, shaping the largest construction project humanity had ever seen.

Then came the animals. Every kind, two by two, trooping aboard with patience modern zookeepers would envy. The imagery is so astonishing that we hardly stop to question the logistics. How do you herd giraffes up a gangplank? What do you feed a lion for forty days at sea? How do you keep the rabbits from multiplying too enthusiastically? We will not get into such details, perhaps wisely, but one can imagine Noah's sons running ragged trying to keep elephants from trampling the hens while goats chewed through the grain stores.

Once all was ready including Noah's family, the animals, and the stores of food, then the skies broke open. Rain fell, not in a gentle patter, but in sheets, torrents, cascades. It was as if the earth itself had decided it had had enough and was joining the rebellion. For forty days and forty nights, water claimed supremacy. Valleys vanished, hills disappeared, and mountains shrank beneath the flood. The world was unmade, not back into nothingness but into a vast, churning sea.

Inside the ark, life must have been a peculiar mixture of monotony and chaos. Imagine the noise. The bellowing of oxen, the braying of donkeys, the bleating of sheep, the squawking of birds. Imagine the smell, even with Noah's best efforts. Imagine the sense of waiting, of being adrift on a world with no landmarks left, only the endless expanse of water. Day blurred into night, night into day, with no stars visible, and no sun clears behind the storm clouds. It must have felt less like surviving and more like floating in a cosmic limbo, suspended between old creation and new.

And then, at last, the rain ceased. The ark drifted in silence, carried by currents no one could chart. Slowly, imperceptibly, the waters began to subside. Peaks began to poke through like the backs of whales breaking the surface. The ark came to rest on the mountains of Ararat, lodged there like a stranded whale itself. But Noah did not fling open the doors straightaway. He waited. He sent out a raven, which flew back and forth until the waters dried. He sent out a dove, which returned empty-beaked, then again, next time returning with a fresh olive leaf, and finally a third time, not returning at all. Only then did Noah open the ark, step out onto firm ground, and breathe the air of a remade world.

What followed was an act of gratitude. Noah built an altar, offering sacrifice in thanks for survival, for mercy, for the chance to begin again. And God, in turn, set a bow in the sky, a rainbow, shimmering across the clouds, as a sign of covenant. Never again, God promised, would a flood of such scale wipe the slate clean. The world, battered but renewed, was given back to humanity.

It is tempting to treat this as the end of the story, a neat conclusion. But in truth it is only the beginning of a new chapter. The flood had cleansed, yes, but it had not cured. Humanity, even in its second chance, would still carry the same restlessness, the same brilliance and folly, the same capacity for both worship and violence. Noah stepped onto dry land as a survivor, but also as the ancestor of every subsequent triumph and tragedy the human story would contain.

And so, the flood ebbs, the rainbow gleams, the ark stands abandoned on its mountain slope, and the earth lies open again, fresh and waiting. A new world, yet the same old humanity.

Chapter Six - Babel and the scattering of nations

After the flood, when the waters subsided and Noah's family stepped onto dry land, there was, for a brief moment, the sense of a fresh chapter. The world was clean again, the slate wiped, and people had a chance to make something of themselves without the long shadow of corruption. And at first, it seemed promising. Noah's descendants multiplied, spread across fields and valleys, learned once more to plough and plant, to herd and to build.

But, as ever, with growth came ambition. It began innocently enough, people wanted to stay together. The memory of the flood was still fresh, and one can hardly blame them for feeling that safety lay in numbers. They journeyed east and settled on a broad plain in Shinar, a place of wide horizons and rich soil. Here, they decided, was where humanity could truly plant its flag.

The innovation of the hour was brick-making. Stone, though durable, was inconveniently scattered and required a great deal of hauling. Bricks, however, could be baked in kilns and stacked neatly, uniform as soldiers. With tar for mortar, whole structures could rise, taller and sturdier than anything yet seen. You can almost hear the pride in their voices: "Come, let us build ourselves a city, with a tower that reaches to the heavens, so that we may make a name for ourselves."

It was not enough to live, to farm, to herd, to sing songs around the fire. Humanity wanted to touch the sky. And so they set to work, an entire civilisation's energy poured into one audacious building project. The Tower of Babel was less about architecture than psychology. It was the first skyscraper, the first monument to human ambition, the first collective attempt to say: "We are here, and we matter."

The problem, of course, was not the bricks or the tower. It was the motive. When humanity clustered together in arrogance and violence, things went very badly indeed. Now, instead of scattering and filling the earth as they had been told, the people of Babel were centralising their pride into a single monument, their ambition stacked layer by layer into the clouds.

God saw the city and the tower. What God saw was not merely masonry, but the direction of humanity's heart. If this was what people could do with one language and one purpose, what else might they attempt? It was not their skill that was dangerous, but their intent.

And so, with a stroke of subtlety rather than thunderbolts, God acted. No flood, no fire, no shattering of stone. Instead it was confusion. Languages multiplied. Words tangled. Orders shouted across scaffolding suddenly made no sense. Where one worker called for more bricks, another heard a request for straw, while a third responded in syllables no one else recognised. Misunderstandings mounted, tempers flared, work ground to a halt. The great tower stood unfinished, a monument not to human triumph but to divine interruption.

From there, humanity scattered. Families and clans drifted apart, not from choice but from necessity, each taking with them their newly minted languages, their own words for sky, for river, for bread, for fire. Nations were born, cultures began, and the world grew diverse in a single stroke. What had been one voice became a chorus, sometimes harmonious, often dissonant, but always varied.

And so the Tower of Babel became the symbol not of reaching the heavens, but of why heaven and earth are never easily reconciled. It marked the end of one kind of unity and the beginning of another story entirely, the tale of tribes and peoples, of languages and borders, of a humanity that would from now on live scattered, never again so entirely united in voice or vision.

Yet, for all its irony, the scattering was not simply a punishment. Diversity is as much gift as it is complication. From it came the richness of cultures, the colours of traditions, the songs and stories that would one day populate every corner of the globe. Humanity lost the tower, but gained the world.

And somewhere amid the confusion of Babel, amid the collapse of its great project, the next thread of the story quietly begins. For out of the scattered nations, out of the sprawl of clans and tongues, one family will be called to begin something new. A man named Abram, from Ur of the Chaldeans, will step forward. And with him will come promises, covenants, and the next chapter in the long and winding chronicle of humanity and God.

Chapter Seven - God's call of Abraham

If the Tower of Babel was humanity's great attempt to climb to heaven, the story of Abraham begins with heaven reaching down to one man. It's a curious shift. Moving from grand strokes, worlds made and unmade, families multiplying, floods swallowing mountains. And now, almost suddenly, we zoom in on one family in one city in Mesopotamia. From here on, things will begin to feel more personal, more intimate.

The man in question was Abram, son of Terah, a native of Ur of the Chaldeans. Ur, in its day, was not some dusty backwater. It was a thriving city-state, perched along the Euphrates, home to temples, merchants, scribes, and the sort of bustle you would expect in a civilisation that knew a thing or two about commerce and irrigation. Abram likely grew up surrounded by the smell of baked clay, the bleating of livestock herded through market squares, the chanting of priests to gods who had names for every mood and season. Life was settled, predictable, rich with tradition.

And then came the voice. Unexpected, uninvited and unsettling. A command so audacious it might have been laughable: "Leave your country, your people, and your father's household, and go to the land I will show you." No destination given, no map provided, only a promise of land, descendants, and blessing. "I will make you into a great nation," God said, "and all peoples on earth will be blessed through you."

It is worth pausing here to consider the scale of what was asked. Abram was not a restless teenager looking for adventure. He was seventy-five, an age when most men are thinking about handing down tools, not packing them up. He was married to Sarai, who by this point had no children and no likelihood of having them. And yet, against all common sense, Abram believed. He gathered his household, his flocks, his servants, and set out from Ur toward a horizon he had never seen.

The journey was long, a slow trudge with dust in the mouth and aching feet. First they travelled northward to Haran, where Terah, his father, eventually died. Then further southwest, into the land of Canaan. He continued to Shechem, Bethel, and the Negev, but behind each stop was the enormity of what it meant to leave everything familiar behind. Imagine pitching a tent beneath unfamiliar stars, wondering if this was the place, only to hear again the whisper "not yet, keep going."

When Abram finally arrived in Canaan, God appeared to him with words of reassurance: "To your offspring I will give this land." Offspring! Abram must have almost laughed at the impossibility. Yet he built an altar there, marking the promise with stones piled high, a gesture of trust in a future he could not yet see.

What follows in Abram's story is a tapestry of faith and fumbling, of bold trust and very human missteps. Famine drove him into Egypt, where, fearing for his life, he passed Sarai off as his sister, a half-truth that caused no end of trouble. Wealth increased, quarrels arose between his herdsmen and those of his nephew Lot, forcing them to part ways. And through it all, God's promise hung in the air like a stubborn refrain: descendants as numerous as the stars, land for them to dwell in, blessing that would ripple outward to every nation.

At night, under the clear sky of Canaan, Abram looked up at the stars, countless and cold. He had no child, no heir, only a gnawing awareness of his and Sarai's age. And yet he believed. Somehow, in the gap between promise and reality, Abram chose trust. He believed the Lord, and it was credited to him as righteousness.

This, then, is the beginning of something entirely new. Out of the scatter of nations, out of the confusion of Babel, God calls one man to begin a story that will run like a golden thread through the rest of history. From Abram will come Isaac, and Jacob, and twelve tribes, and eventually a people set apart. From his line will come kings and prophets, songs and laws, exiles and returns. Also from his seed will one day come the fulfilment of the oldest promise of all.

But for now, Abram is simply a man with a tent, a wife, and a promise. He wanders the land of Canaan, an outsider among its inhabitants, marking his path with altars, carrying with him a voice that will not be silenced.

It is, in its way, the greatest gamble in history. One man stepping out into the unknown, trusting that the God who made the heavens and the earth also keeps his word. And from that gamble, a nation and eventually a faith was born.

To picture Abraham, or Abram as he was still called then, you must imagine a man on the move. His life became a rhythm of pitching and striking tents, of searching for pasture, of never quite belonging anywhere. The land of Canaan was already filled with tribes who had their own languages, customs, and loyalties. To them, Abram was a stranger, one of those curious wandering clans that passed through with goats and camels, staying long enough to graze the fields before vanishing into the hills again.

Nomadic life had its peculiar hardships. Food was never taken for granted. Water was always a calculation, a daily arithmetic of survival. Every dawn began with the same chores of herdsmen driving bleating flocks to graze, women pounding grain, the smoke of fires curling into the pale light. Abram moved through it all with a staff in hand and that nagging voice in the back of his mind reminding him of the promise.

The promise was a double-edged gift. On the one hand, it gave him purpose, a sense that these wanderings were not just the meaningless shuffle of survival but steps on a journey towards something greater. On the other, it was maddening. Years passed, and Sarai's belly stayed flat. Years passed, and the land he was promised remained firmly in the hands of others. At times it must have felt like walking in circles under a sky full of stars that glittered with possibilities just out of reach.

And yet, Abram was not without comforts. He was wealthy by the standards of his world with flocks, silver, servants, and all the practical wealth of a man with influence. His camp was not a ragtag scattering of tents but a small travelling village. He had men trained for battle, enough to march into a fight and win. This was not the life of a starving wanderer but of a leader moving cautiously through foreign lands, wealthy enough to be noticed, vulnerable enough to be nervous.

Everywhere Abram went, he built altars. Small piles of stone, unremarkable to outsiders, but to him they were anchors of memory. In Shechem, Bethel, and Hebron the stones still spoke long after the campfires were cold, testifying that in this place God had appeared, or spoken, or promised. These were not grand ziggurats like the ones he had seen in Ur. They were simple, personal monuments, more like cairns left by a hiker marking the trail than shrines designed to impress. They were there to remind him that all this wandering was not without direction.

Then there was Egypt, a curious detour brought on by famine. The fertile Nile valley must have been a shock after the dry hills of Canaan. Egypt in Abram's day was already ancient, with its stone temples, hieroglyphs carved deep into walls, and officials who thought in terms of dynasties while Abram thought in terms of tents. It was here he faltered, fearing that Sarai's beauty might tempt someone to kill him. He tried to protect himself by passing her off as his sister, which led to Pharaoh's house being thrown into turmoil by plagues until the truth came out. Abram left Egypt richer than before, but perhaps chastened by the reminder that trusting God was not a part-time exercise.

Back in Canaan, the quarrels with Lot arose. Both men had prospered, their herds swelling to the point where the land could not support them together. Herdsmen argued, tempers flared, and Abram, ever the peacemaker, offered Lot the first choice of land. Lot chose the lush Jordan valley, the well-watered plain near Sodom, leaving Abram the hill country. It seemed at the time like Abram had accepted the lesser share. But soon after, God renewed the promise, telling him to look north, south, east, and west, for all of it would one day belong to his descendants.

At night, when the campfires burned low and Sarai lay beside him, Abram would sometimes slip outside, look up at the uncountable stars, and wonder. Was he a fool to believe? Was this all just a mad wandering, one more tribe chasing after visions in the desert? Or was he truly on the threshold of something greater? He had no son, no heir, nothing tangible to show for the years of moving from one rocky outcrop to another. And yet he believed. Not perfectly, his story is full of falters and fixes, but enough to keep walking.

And so Abram wandered, never quite settling, never quite belonging, but always carrying within him the astonishing thought that the Creator of the universe had spoken his name.

Chapter Eight - Isaac, Jacob, and the promises

The story of Abraham is not simply about a man, but about a promise stubborn enough to stretch across generations. The problem with promises, however, is that they often take far longer to materialise than we'd like. By the time Abraham and Sarah finally had a child, both were old enough to be thinking about slippers and shawls, not new-born nappies and night feeds. Yet the child came, and his very name was laughter. His name was Isaac.

Now, in the ancient Near East, names carried more weight than in our own world, where we mostly choose them because they sound nice, fit a celebrity trend, or remind us of a great aunt. Isaac's name, meaning "he laughs," was a monument to the absurdity of it all, the ridiculousness of a hundred-year-old man bouncing a baby on his knee, the incredulity of Sarah who had once laughed at the suggestion but now laughed for joy. Every time the boy's name was called across the camp, it was a reminder of divine humour and human disbelief turned on its head.

Isaac's life, compared to Abraham's, was quieter, less dramatic, almost pastoral in its rhythm. Whereas Abraham had been called out of a city to become a wanderer, Isaac was born into the wandering life and knew nothing else. He dug wells, reopened his father's old ones, and lived in that same precarious balance of trust and survival. He, too, faced famine and detoured into foreign lands. He, too, experienced the unease of being a stranger in someone else's territory. Yet his story lacks the fireworks of his father's. Abraham was the pioneer and Sarah the matriarch, Isaac was the caretaker, keeping the promise alive not through bold adventures but through steady continuity.

It is worth remembering that the great story often advances not through astonishing acts of heroism but through the sheer dogged persistence of people simply carrying the promise forward. Isaac was not a figure of thunder and drama. He was a bridge, a link in the chain, the living proof that God's word had not failed.

But then comes Jacob, and here things become more lively. Isaac is quiet water, Jacob is a stream full of bends, trickles, and the occasional mischievous splash. Born the younger twin to Esau, Jacob arrived clutching his brother's heel, as if from the very start he intended to wrestle his way into blessings not technically his. His name meant "supplanter," and he lived up to it with gusto.

Jacob's story is one of scheming and scrambling, but also of encounters with the divine that changed him in ways he never anticipated. First came the episode of the birthright. Esau, red and ruddy, a hunter with the appetite to match, came back famished from the field. Jacob, ever opportunistic, offered him stew in exchange for his inheritance as the firstborn. Esau, in a moment of hunger-induced carelessness, agreed. And so the younger brother, with one bowl of lentils, outmanoeuvred the elder.

Later came the deception of their father. Isaac, old and nearly blind, prepared to give Esau his final blessing. Jacob, egged on by his mother Rebekah, disguised himself in goat skins to mimic his hairy brother and tricked Isaac into blessing him instead. It was, to put it mildly, a family scandal. Esau's fury burned hot, and Jacob fled for his life, setting in motion a lifetime of wandering that made even Abraham's look tame.

On his way into exile, Jacob stopped for the night and lay down with a stone for a pillow. It was there, under the open sky that he dreamed of a ladder, or perhaps a stairway, reaching from earth to heaven, with angels moving up and down it like couriers between worlds. At the top of the ladder stood the Lord reaffirming the ancient promise. The promise of land, descendants, and the blessing to all nations. When Jacob awoke, startled and wide-eyed, he declared, "Surely the Lord is in this place, and I was not aware of it." He set up a stone as a marker and called the place Bethel, the "house of God." For Jacob, who had schemed his way into blessings, this was a reminder that some promises come not by trickery but by grace.

His years away were filled with irony. In Haran he met his match in Laban, his uncle, who tricked him into marrying Leah instead of Rachel, forcing him into fourteen years of labour for the two sisters he loved unequally. The trickster was tricked, the supplanter supplanted. Yet through it all, his household grew. Children arrived, twelve sons in all, each destined to become the ancestor of a tribe. The promise of countless descendants was taking visible shape, if not without a good deal of domestic chaos.

When Jacob finally left Laban and made his way back toward Canaan, he dreaded meeting Esau again. He sent flocks ahead as peace offerings, divided his camp for safety, and spent a restless night by the river Jabbok. There, in the deep dark, he wrestled with a stranger till dawn, an encounter so strange it has defied explanation ever since. Was it an angel? Was it God himself? Was it Jacob wrestling with his own fears and guilt? Jacob limped away at sunrise, blessed but wounded, renamed Israel, "he struggles with God."

That limp would define him as much as the blessing. Jacob, who had spent his life grasping heels and outmanoeuvring brothers, discovered that the promises of God were not prizes to be stolen but gifts to be wrestled with, lived with, and sometimes limped away from. His children, a rowdy and quarrelsome lot, would carry the name Israel, and their descendants would inherit not only land but this strange calling to struggle with God and yet be chosen by him.

Isaac and Jacob's stories remind us that divine promises rarely unfold in straight lines. They twist through laughter and deception, through stew and stone pillows, through weddings that went sideways and brothers who held grudges. Yet through it all, the promise remained intact. The God who had spoken to Abraham in the open sky continued to weave his purposes through the quirks and quarrels of this family.

And so the family became a nation in seed form. Abraham the pioneer, Isaac the bridge, and Jacob the struggler. Three men, three lives, and three ways of carrying the promise forward. Behind them, altars of stone. Before them, generations yet unborn.

Chapter Nine - Joseph and Israel in Egypt

Jacob, now called Israel, was the father of twelve sons, each of whom would give his name to a tribe. That sounds orderly, almost like someone sat down with a family-planning chart and said, "Right, twelve it is, one for each future tribe, done and dusted." The reality was anything but orderly. It was the story of one man, two wives, two concubines, and more sibling rivalry than a soap opera writer could ever hope for.

Leah, unloved but fruitful, gave Jacob son after son, each name a small cry for recognition. Reuben, "See, a son!" as if to say, "Now my husband will notice me." Simeon, "Because the Lord heard" a hint of longing in her choice. Levi, "Attached" her hope that Jacob might finally cling to her. Judah, "Praise" her attempt to lift her eyes beyond her own ache. Meanwhile Rachel, Jacob's beloved, remained barren, fuming as her sister's tent filled with children. She handed Jacob her maid Bilhah, who produced two more sons. Leah, not to be outdone, countered with her own maid Zilpah, who produced sons in turn. The household became a competitive childbearing contest, complete with bitter words, awkward arrangements, and children who grew up knowing they were pawns in their mothers' rivalries.

Rachel, at last, had her own miracle child. Her son Joseph was born after years of waiting, the apple of Jacob's eye. Later came Benjamin, her second, but at the cost of her life in childbirth. Her death left Jacob with grief stitched into the very fabric of his joy.

Reuben, Simeon, Levi, Judah, Dan, Naphtali, Gad, Asher, Issachar, Zebulun, Joseph, and Benjamin were hardly paragons of virtue. They bickered, schemed, and occasionally did things so appalling that one wonders how any nation could possibly be founded on such a crew. And yet these were the men through whom the promise would flow, flawed as they were.

The most famous among them, of course, was Joseph, the dreamer. Jacob, unable to hide his favouritism, gave him a richly ornamented robe that might as well have been a neon sign flashing, "Favourite child." His brothers, predictably, seethed. Joseph didn't help matters by sharing dreams in which his brothers bowed before him. You can imagine how well that went down over breakfast.

Resentment boiled over when Joseph was sent to check on his brothers in the fields. They plotted to kill him, then downgraded the plan to selling him to passing traders. It was an act of betrayal so chilling in its coldness that later generations would look back and shudder. They dipped his robe in goat's blood and showed it to their father, who collapsed into inconsolable grief. Jacob tore his clothes, wept, and refused comfort, believing his favourite son to have been devoured by wild beasts.

Joseph, meanwhile, was carted off to Egypt, a slave in a foreign land, his dreams seemingly shattered. But here the great irony of the promise comes into play. The God who had guided Abraham out of Ur and Jacob back to Canaan was also with Joseph in the pits of slavery and the false accusations of prison. Each setback became another step to something astonishing.

While Joseph languished in Egypt, the brothers returned home and carried their secret like a stone in the gut. They watched their father wither under grief, each of them knowing the truth but saying nothing. It is remarkable, really, how long guilt can simmer unspoken, shaping lives in quiet, corrosive ways.

Yet through Joseph, Egypt became the unlikely stage where the promise would stretch its wings.

Initially, Joseph served in the house of Potiphar, an officer of Pharaoh. He was diligent, intelligent, and, importantly, trustworthy. Within a short time, he rose to a position of authority, overseeing Potiphar's household. Everything seemed to be going smoothly, too smoothly, perhaps. For Joseph, it turns out that nothing in life comes without its shadow. Potiphar's wife noticed the handsome foreigner and tried to seduce him. Joseph, loyal and upright, resisted. But his refusal only led to a new trial with a false accusation. He was cast into prison, betrayed not by his brothers this time but by the moral rigor that defined him.

The prison, grim and dark, might have seemed the end, yet even there Joseph's life demonstrates the strange logic of providence. He quickly gained the trust of the warden, interpreting dreams for fellow prisoners, including Pharaoh's cupbearer and baker. For two years, he languished in jail until the moment fates were required for a larger plan. Joseph's skill with dreams was incredible and he could read the symbols and images with precision, seeing not only personal fortunes but the sweep of years to come.

The turning point came when Pharaoh himself dreamed of cows, seven healthy, seven gaunt and grain, abundant and then ravaged. No one could interpret these visions. The cupbearer, suddenly recalling Joseph's gift, mentioned him to Pharaoh. Joseph, summoned, interpreted the dreams with uncanny clarity. Seven years of plenty would be followed by seven years of famine. More than that, he offered a solution, a plan to store surplus grain during the years of abundance, to weather the coming scarcity.

Pharaoh, impressed and awed, elevated Joseph to the highest rank short of Pharaoh himself. He became vizier, master of Egypt's storehouses, and overseer of all lands in preparation for famine. Joseph, once a slave, now commanded the destiny of an empire. The same brothers who had thrown him into a pit now would come, unknowingly, seeking food in a land he ruled.

And here is where the story becomes almost unbearably human. Joseph recognised them immediately, but they did not recognise him. Joseph, in a remarkable act of self-restraint, chose testing over immediate retribution. He accused them of being spies, detained them, and orchestrated a series of tense encounters to observe their character, to see whether guilt had softened into repentance.

The tension was unbearable. Brothers trembled, hearts pounded, and Jacob, back in Canaan, fretted at the slow return of his sons. Meanwhile, Joseph's dreams, the very visions that had once made him a target, were being fulfilled in ways no one could have foreseen. Eventually, he revealed himself, not with a yell of triumph but with tears, a statement of forgiveness, and the invitation for his family to settle in Egypt. "I am Joseph," he said. "Is my father still alive?" He embraced Benjamin, his youngest brother, and the family wept together in a reunion both joyous and poignant.

Pharaoh, hearing of Joseph's family, welcomed them. He provided the land of Goshen, fertile and isolated enough for the family to thrive without interference. Jacob and his sons settled there, flocks and herds multiplying, tents rising, the promise of Abraham quietly taking root once more, though under foreign skies. Egypt, land of pyramids and Pharaohs, became home, not as conquerors, but as guests, nurtured by divine provision.

Jacob, in his final years, took stock of the generations. Each son received his blessing, words weighted with prophecy and reflection. Some were straightforward, others cryptic. Some praised courage, others foretold future struggles. The tribes of Israel were sketched in miniature, each personality a thread in the larger tapestry. And Jacob, blessed and worn, passed on with the knowledge that his family would continue, that promises made to Abraham were now secured through generations, and that even in exile, destiny moves quietly forward.

Joseph, too, lived to witness the unfolding of these promises. He reassured his brothers, foretelling that God had sent him ahead to preserve life. He died as he had lived. He was a man of vision, resilience, and faith, entombed in Egypt but with the assurance that the journey of his descendants would eventually return them to the land promised long ago.

In Goshen, a nation began to stir in seed form. From a single family, fugitives, wanderers, tricksters, and dreamers emerged a people who would carry forward the covenant, the promise that Abraham's descendants would be as numerous as the stars, land, and blessing. It was the slow, patient work of God, woven through deception and fidelity, hardship and triumph, betrayal and forgiveness.

And so the story of Joseph and Israel in Egypt stands as a bridge between the wanderings of Abraham and Jacob, and the coming epic of exodus and liberation.

Chapter Ten - Moses and the burning bush

Moses came from the tribe of Levi. He was a descendent of one of Jacob's twelve sons. Moses' father, Amram, was a Levite, and his mother, Jochebed, was also from the Levite line, making Moses a direct descendant of Levi. It is important to mention that marriages within extended families were common to preserve lineage and tribal inheritance.

The Hebrews, who were Moses' own people, had been enslaved in Egypt. They were living under harsh conditions imposed by Pharaoh, who feared their numbers and strength. His decree was simple and brutal. Every new born Hebrew boy was to be thrown into the Nile. The logic of the ruler was grimly practical, if the boys survived, they would grow into soldiers and threats. If they did not, the problem was solved.

Into this perilous world, Moses was born to the Levite couple who were themselves already navigating the treacherous currents of survival. Amram, part of a tribe set apart for priestly duties, would have known the precariousness of life in Egypt, the tension between assimilation and faithfulness. Jochebed, described as resourceful and courageous, took matters into her own hands when it became clear that the infant Moses' life was in danger.

From the moment of his birth, Moses' survival was a small miracle. Jochebed placed him in a basket, woven from bulrushes and coated with pitch and tar to make it waterproof, and set it among the reeds along the banks of the Nile. One can picture her as she did this, heart pounding, whispering prayers under her breath, hands trembling, aware that each moment of delay could mean disaster. The basket was both protection and risk, a tiny vessel carrying the fragile future of a man who would one day confront Pharaoh and lead a nation.

It was Pharaoh's daughter, while bathing in the river, who discovered the basket. She saw the crying infant, the helpless bundle, and felt compassion. Against the king's edict, she chose to rescue him. Here is one of those small, almost human moments in biblical history. A princess sees an abandoned child and makes a personal decision that would ripple across generations. She named him Moses, which can be understood as "drawn out" (from the water), a fitting name for a life literally pulled from danger.

Moses' early years were spent in the royal palace, a young man raised with privileges most Hebrews could scarcely imagine including fine linens, tutors, the subtleties of courtly life, the politics of power, and the etiquette of the Egyptian elite. Yet he also carried within him a secret identity, he had discovered that he was Hebrew, part of the enslaved people who sang in the fields and laboured under the sun. That duality, privilege and heritage, palace and oppression, shaped him profoundly.

Even as a boy, Moses likely observed the suffering around him and the long hours of forced labour, the cries of workers, the oppression of the people. One can imagine him walking along the Nile, seeing Hebrew children like himself, and feeling a stirring of justice, a quiet, growing awareness that he could not be indifferent. It was a seed planted early, nurtured by both family loyalty and the moral tension of living in two worlds.

Moses also had siblings, Aaron and Miriam, who would become essential figures in his life. Miriam, his older sister, showed remarkable courage even in infancy, watching over him when he floated in the basket and later helping to reunite him with his mother as a nurse. Aaron, destined to be his spokesperson, his partner in leadership, was born into this same precarious and charged environment, setting the stage for the sibling relationships that would later shape the Exodus.

Moses was a child that was hidden from death and raised in luxury, yet shadowed by the plight of his people. The experience of living between worlds, of seeing oppression first hand while enjoying privileges not afforded to his people. This honed in Moses a keen sense of justice and responsibility. It also prepared him, unknowingly, for the burdens of leadership.

By the time Moses reached adulthood, he had the knowledge of Egypt and the heart of a Hebrew. This dual perspective would prove crucial, he understood Pharaoh's court, the workings of power, the subtleties of influence, but he also understood the suffering of the people, their cries, their hopes, and their fears. The stage was set for a man who would not simply inherit a promise but become the instrument through which God's promises would be fulfilled.

And thus, the child who floated among the reeds, who was drawn from the water, grew into a man whose destiny would take him far from palace walls into deserts, confrontations with kings, miraculous signs, and a burning bush that would change the course of history forever.

The sight of his people suffering and bending under the yoke of oppression had ignited a visceral anger within him. This resulted in a turning point when Moses came upon an Egyptian taskmaster striking a Hebrew slave. Moses acted, violently and decisively, killing the overseer and hiding the body in the sand. In that single, impulsive act, the careful, educated prince of Egypt collided with the Hebrew boy in him. It was an inflection in his life that would send him tumbling into exile.

Pharaoh, unsurprisingly, heard of the incident. Moses, once beloved in the court, became a fugitive overnight. He fled Egypt, crossing the desert, leaving behind the comfort and predictability of palace life for the uncertain expanses of the wilderness. For a man accustomed to stone walls, fine linens, and regular meals, the desert must have felt both terrifying and starkly beautiful with endless horizons, sun-baked earth, nights of piercing cold, and a sky strewn with stars. This was a world where survival depended on ingenuity, patience, and endurance, not on birthright or privilege.

Moses wandered into Midian, a rugged, sparsely populated region of hills and valleys, and here he found work tending flocks for Jethro (also called Reuel), the priest of Midian. The life of a shepherd was humbling and formative. Each day was long, measured by the rise and fall of the sun, by the rhythm of the flocks. Moses learned patience while practicing the quiet art of guiding sheep, protecting them from predators, finding water in a harsh land. He learned observation by noticing subtle shifts in the weather, tracking animal movements, reading the patterns of the land. And he learned solitude with the hours and days spent alone with his thoughts, pondering life, justice, and his place in the world.

It was a far cry from the bustling courts of Egypt. Yet in this simplicity, Moses grew stronger and not only physically, but also spiritually and mentally. The desert is an unforgiving teacher, and a shepherd's life demands vigilance and humility. For years, he became intimately familiar with the land, the seasons, and the delicate balance between danger and survival. It is easy to imagine him leaning on a staff at twilight, gazing at the horizon, thinking of his people in Egypt, feeling both guilt and longing, and dreaming of a life that might be more than just survival.

During this time, Moses married Zipporah, Jethro's daughter. The marriage tied him to a community and gave him a family of his own. Raising children, tending flocks, and navigating tribal dynamics sharpened his leadership, teaching him diplomacy, responsibility, and the patience required to manage both people and livestock. The seeds of the leader he would become were planted in the quiet rhythms of Midianite hills, watered by long years of reflection and modest work.

It is in this context that the burning bush appears. The moment is electric precisely because it interrupts a life that has grown routine. He is called not in the palace, not in Egypt, not in triumph or ceremony, but in the desert, tending flocks on holy ground. The bush burns, yet is not consumed, and God speaks directly to him. The years in Midian, the exile, the solitude, the humility all converge to prepare Moses for this encounter. He has learned to listen, to act with discernment, to trust in a power larger than himself.

The flight into Midian, then, is not merely an escape from danger. It is a formative journey. It strips Moses of privilege, teaches him resilience, patience, and observation, and positions him to hear God's call. The burning bush would never have the same meaning for a man untested by hardship, unshaped by solitude, or unacquainted with the suffering of others. By the time he stands before it, he is ready, not as a boy of the palace, not as a fugitive, but as a shepherd, a husband, and a man whose life has been quietly honed for a moment that will change history.

Moses was tending the flocks of Jethro in the Midianite hills and noticed a bush flickering with flames against the muted browns and greens of the wilderness. It burned, yet it was not consumed. Imagine that, fire dancing and crackling, the smell of smoke perhaps faint, yet the bush itself remaining fully alive, green, vibrant. He leaned closer, curiosity pulling him as if by invisible hands.

And then he heard a voice, clear and commanding, calling his name. "Moses! Moses!" Startled, he froze. Here, in the quiet desert came a voice that held authority, presence, and warmth all at once. "Do not come any closer," the voice continued. "Take off your sandals, for the place where you stand is holy ground."

This was no everyday encounter. The burning bush was a threshold, a liminal space. Moses, a man shaped by palace intrigue, shepherd solitude, exile, and observation, now stood in the presence of God, and the ground itself was sacred. He removed his sandals, feeling the rough earth beneath his feet, aware that the world had just shifted in an instant.

God spoke of suffering and promise. "I have seen the affliction of my people in Egypt," the voice said. "I have heard their cries and come to deliver them. I am sending you to Pharaoh to bring my people out of Egypt." Moses' first response was naturally hesitation. He was a man who had spent decades in a quiet desert, tending sheep, far from the intrigues of kings. Who am I, he asked, to confront Pharaoh and to lead a nation?

God, patient and reassuring, offered signs: a staff that becomes a serpent, a hand that becomes leprous and then restored, and the promise of divine presence. Even then, Moses protested further that he was not eloquent, he feared rejection, and he feared failure. God appointed Aaron, Moses' brother, as his spokesperson, acknowledging human limitations while demonstrating that the mission's power lay not in Moses alone but in God's guidance.

The burning bush is full of paradox. Fire, which normally destroys, here illuminates without consuming. Moses, a shepherd who had learned patience, humility, and observation, is called not by circumstance but by a direct, personal summons. His years in exile had not been wasted, rather they had prepared him to hear, understand, and act upon the divine call.

Chapter Eleven - The Exodus from Egypt

Moses came down from Mount Horeb changed. The quiet shepherd who had spent years among sheep and hills now carried a fire in his chest. The memory of the burning bush lingered, not only in his mind but in his bones, as if some of its unconsuming flame had lodged within him. Yet for all that, his steps back toward Egypt must have been heavy. Returning to the land he had fled, the palace he had abandoned, the people he had left behind. There was dread, guilt, uncertainty, but also a strange, unshakable sense of purpose.

His first reunion was with his brother Aaron was not just a family moment but the beginning of a partnership that would define the Exodus. Aaron, older, steadier, more articulate, would serve as Moses' voice. Together, they would face Pharaoh, the ruler of Egypt, the man who was considered semi-divine, the absolute power in a land that measured time in dynasties.

When Moses and Aaron first stood before Pharaoh, the encounter must have been both daunting and surreal. In the grand hall, stone pillars rising high, walls painted with scenes of gods and victories, the air thick with incense, Pharaoh on his throne, surrounded by priests, scribes, and guards. Into this atmosphere of splendour and intimidation walked two

Hebrew men, desert-dressed, holding nothing but a staff and a story of a God Pharaoh did not know.

Their request was simple in wording but monumental in meaning: "Let my people go." It was not a plea for kindness, but a declaration of divine command. Pharaoh's reaction was predictable. He laughed, scoffed, or perhaps stared in disdain. Why should he obey? Why should the most powerful man in the world bend to the demands of shepherds? Instead of relenting, Pharaoh tightened his grip. He increased the burdens of the Hebrew slaves. Liberation had been demanded, and oppression grew worse.

And so began the long, escalating struggle which was a clash not only between Moses and Pharaoh, but between the God of Israel and the gods of Egypt.

The first signs from God seemed almost like performances of magic. Pharaoh's magicians managed to mimic some of these signs, shrugging them off as clever tricks. But the demonstrations escalated.

The Nile, which was the source of Egypt's life and fertility, turned to blood, stinking with dead fish. Frogs emerged in absurd numbers, hopping into houses, kitchens, and even into Pharaoh's bedchamber. Dust turned to gnats, swarming across the land, filling eyes and noses. Then came flies, in such numbers that Egypt buzzed and crawled with them.

With each plague, the disruption grew more serious, and Pharaoh's defiance hardened.

Livestock fell sick and died, crippling Egypt's economy. Boils erupted on human and animal skin alike, painful and humiliating. Then the skies themselves seemed to turn against Pharaoh as hailstones pummelled the land, smashing crops and trees, followed by locusts that devoured whatever green remained. Finally, darkness spread over Egypt for three days, a thick, oppressive night that extinguished even the confidence of the priests of Ra, the sun-god.

Each plague was more than a punishment but rather a symbolic dismantling of Egypt's pantheon and pride. The Nile, frogs, livestock, sun were all were deities in the Egyptian worldview, and here they were shown powerless before the God of Israel.

Yet Pharaoh's heart remained stubborn. Sometimes he seemed to relent, only to change his mind once relief came. It was a deadly tug-of-war, with the lives and freedom of the Hebrews hanging in the balance.

The last plague was the most devastating. It was not spectacle, but sorrow. It was the death of the firstborn. From Pharaoh's heir to the child of the lowliest servant, from human households to the stalls of cattle, the firstborn of Egypt were struck down in a single night. The cries of grief rose across the land, the sound of a nation mourning.

But for the Hebrews, there was protection. They were commanded to sacrifice a lamb, mark their doorposts with its blood, and eat a hurried meal, roasted meat, unleavened bread, and bitter herbs in order to be ready for a journey. This was the first Passover, a meal of both fear and hope, eaten with sandals on feet and staffs in hand, as death passed by their protected homes.

Pharaoh, broken at last, called Moses and Aaron and told them to go, go with their people, go with their flocks, go and never return. After generations of bondage, the Hebrews walked out of Egypt, a vast throng moving under the desert sky, carrying with them not only their possessions but the memory of deliverance.

It was not however the end of Pharaoh's resistance. His armies would pursue, leading to the drama of the Red Sea. But the night of Passover marked the true birth of a people, no longer just a family descended from Jacob, but a nation bound by shared suffering, shared hope, and the promise of freedom.

The burning bush had set this all in motion. A shepherd had become a prophet, a fugitive had become a leader, and the God who had appeared in fire had now revealed Himself in acts of power that shook an empire.

If you picture the Exodus as an orderly march, everyone lined up in neat rows, children holding hands, sheep behaving politely then you are probably imagining something closer to a village fete than the real thing. What actually left Egypt was, by all accounts, an enormous, bewildered crowd of former slaves and their animals, staggering out in a half-celebratory, half-panicked state. Not just Hebrews, but other stragglers, Egyptians, and who-knows-who, all swept up in the momentum of a people on the move.

Now, imagine the logistics. Here were thousands, perhaps hundreds of thousands wandering out of Egypt with little more than flatbread and optimism. They had no road map, no military protection, and their only guide was a God who appeared as a curious combination of cloud by day and fire by night. A travel agency would have called it "adventurous" and declined liability.

Of course, Pharaoh soon realised he'd made a colossal mistake. His free labour force had just marched out of his country, singing songs about freedom. Within days, regret hardened into fury, and he dispatched his army with chariots gleaming, horses pounding, soldiers no doubt muttering about how ridiculous it was to be chasing runaway brickmakers across the desert.

This set up one of the more cinematic chase scenes in human history. On one side, a mass of unarmed ex-slaves, trudging through sand, nervously looking over their shoulders. On the other, the Egyptian war machine, bearing down with the confidence of men who'd never once lost a fight to sheep-herders, and dead ahead was the sea.

Here's where Moses comes into his own. Until now, he had been equal parts reluctant spokesman, amateur negotiator, and somewhat frazzled middle manager trying to corral a restive people. But on the shores of the Red Sea, he becomes something else entirely. The people panic, because what else would you do when the greatest army in the world is at your back and the ocean is up ahead? But Moses, staff in hand, tells them to stand firm. He says they will see deliverance. And then, against all natural expectations, the waters shift.

The image of the Red Sea parting is so familiar that we forget just how strange it must have been to witness. Walls of water on either side, a strip of dry land in the middle, wind roaring like a storm through a canyon of waves. It must have been terrifying. No one had ever walked through a sea before. Imagine being halfway across and glancing up at the water looming beside you, hoping it stayed politely in place. Yet across they went, thousands upon thousands, stumbling, pushing, dragging carts, clutching children, trying not to lose track of which goat belonged to whom.

The Egyptians, of course, followed. Why wouldn't they? If the sea had opened for slaves, surely it would open for chariots. But the crossing wasn't made for them. Once the last Hebrew foot left the seabed, the waters closed back with terrible force, swallowing horses, wheels, armour, and pride. One moment the Egyptians were thundering forward, the next they were gone, the sea restored to its old, untroubled ways, as though nothing had happened at all.

On the far shore, the people must have stood in stunned silence at first, staring at the waves, still hearing the echo of hooves and shouts that had just ceased. Then the relief hit them, they were free, properly free, not just fugitives but survivors. And so they sang. One of the oldest recorded songs in history was composed on that beach, celebrating not just survival but the baffling, improbable fact that they were still alive.

From there, the journey would turn into years of wandering, testing, complaining, and growing, but the Red Sea crossing was the defining moment. It was the day they stopped being runaway slaves and became a people with a story, the people who walked through the sea.

Chapter Twelve - Sinai and the covenant

After the Red Sea, the wilderness became the Israelites' new classroom. And wilderness is a very particular sort of teacher. It does not care about your timetable, your appetite, or your general sense of comfort. It strips you down, pares away illusions, and leaves you with yourself, your companions, and whatever God you have.

So imagine thousands of Israelites trudging through rocky valleys and barren plateaus, grumbling about food, water, and direction. It was, in short, less like a jubilant holiday and more like a badly planned camping trip gone on far too long. Their diet was monotonous, manna in the morning, manna in the evening, and for variety, quail when God decided enough was enough of the complaining. If you want to appreciate the miracle of manna, picture sweet flakes scattered across the desert floor at dawn, delicate as frost. But also picture eating it every single day for forty years. One suspects enthusiasm waned.

All this was building towards Sinai. The mountain rises like a jagged tooth out of the southern desert, a place of stark grandeur, where bare rock meets cloud and wind. Here, in this forbidding environment, God decided to establish something utterly new, not just a rescue, not just survival, but a covenant, a formal, binding agreement that would shape the people's identity forever.

The scene has a kind of volcanic terror. Thunder, lightning, a cloud descending, the mountain trembling as if the whole earth were nervous. The people are warned not to approach too closely, under penalty of death. You can almost see them craning their necks, shielding their eyes, torn between fear and curiosity. And at the centre of it all stands Moses, the unlikely go-between, the man who speaks with God on behalf of an entire nation.

The covenant itself is simple in outline but monumental in meaning. It is a marriage, of sorts, between God and a people. God says, I brought you out of Egypt, I carried you on eagle's wings, and now I will be your God if you will be my people. The people say yes, and agree that everything the Lord has said, they will do.

At Sinai, the Israelites receive the Ten Commandments, the famous set of instructions carved onto stone tablets. And here it's worth pausing, because these aren't random rules about trivialities. They're strikingly concise, surprisingly universal, and oddly practical for people who had just emerged from centuries of servitude. Don't worship other gods, don't carve idols, don't misuse God's name, keep a rhythm of rest, honour your parents, don't kill, don't commit adultery, don't steal, don't lie in court, and don't covet. It's not exhaustive, but it's enough to sketch the outlines of a sane and decent society.

It is fascinating how these commandments combine the vertical (honour God) and the horizontal (treat one another decently). It's not just a matter of piety but a framework for justice, for community life, for the very possibility of living together without tearing each other apart. For a people just learning how to be free, this was their foundation document.

The covenant didn't end with the commandments. There were festivals to mark, laws about restitution and fairness, instructions for worship, and a whole architecture of tabernacle and priesthood to embody God's presence among them. Imagine the camp buzzing with activity. Carpenters measuring wood for sacred furnishings, women weaving curtains of blue and scarlet, metalworkers hammering bronze for altars. It was religion in the making, and also nation-building at its rawest.

And yet, even in the middle of such grandeur, there is the unmissable human comedy. When Moses went up the mountain and stayed rather longer than expected, the people quickly assumed he'd either died or abandoned them. Their solution? Melt down jewellery and build a golden calf to worship. After all, if you're going to invent a new god, why not make it a shiny cow? Moses came down, tablets in hand, only to find the people dancing around their bovine substitute. He smashed the tablets in fury, an act that must have felt cathartic at the time but also meant he had to go back up the mountain for replacements, which can't have been fun.

Sinai is a pivotal point because the Israelites are no longer just escapees, wanderers with a dramatic backstory. They are now bound in covenant. They have a law, a God who travels with them, and a set of obligations that will define them not as individuals but as a people. The desert still lies before them, long and arduous, but their identity has shifted. They are not simply former slaves. They are covenant partners, a people with commandments carved in stone, a people married, as it were, to the divine.

Chapter Thirteen - Wilderness wanderings

If Sinai was a honeymoon, the wilderness was the long, sometimes fractious marriage. Having solemnly pledged themselves to God with a chorus of "All that the Lord has spoken we will do," the Israelites almost immediately began the practice of not doing it. From here on, the story of their desert years reads like a pattern of crisis, complaint, divine response, momentary gratitude, and forgetfulness, repeat.

First, the food. Manna was astonishing, dew-turned-flakes that could be gathered each morning and baked into cakes. Almost like coriander seed, delicate, fine, a kind of edible frost. But after months of eating it, enthusiasm waned. "We remember the fish we ate in Egypt, the cucumbers, the melons, the leeks, the onions, and the garlic," they moaned, in one of history's earliest examples of nostalgia for bad times. Egypt may have been slavery, but at least it had salad.

Water, too, became a recurring drama. At one point, the people were so desperate they accused Moses of leading them into the desert to die of thirst. It is not easy being a leader when your followers would rather be back in chains than thirsty. Moses, exasperated, cried out to God, who instructed him to strike a rock with his staff. Out gushed water, saving the day, though one wonders whether the sheep were quicker to lap it up than the people.

Then there was the matter of meat. God obliged with quail, an improbable mass migration of birds that landed right in the camp. Imagine a community suddenly knee-deep in quail, feathered abundance flapping about in every direction. People gathered them by the basketful, but the whole episode soured quickly, with sickness breaking out, perhaps a reminder that gluttony in the desert is still gluttony.

Beyond food and drink, there was the small matter of organisation. Moses, poor man, was constantly caught between God above and the people below. At one point, his father-in-law Jethro who was visiting from Midian took one look at the chaos and advised him to delegate. "You'll wear yourself out," Jethro said, in what must be one of the earliest recorded management consultations. Judges and leaders were appointed over smaller groups, which probably did wonders for Moses' sanity, if not the people's propensity to argue.

But the wilderness wasn't just about grumbling. It was also a testing ground for trust. God led them by the cloud and fire, taught them rhythms of rest (gather double manna on the sixth day, none on the seventh), and instructed them in how to camp, march, and worship. A portable tabernacle became the focus of divine presence, an elaborate tent with gilded furnishings and priestly rituals, a kind of travelling cathedral in the desert. It gave the people a visible centre, a sense of structure, and perhaps reassurance that God was still in their midst even when the journey felt endless.

Still, human nature is wonderfully consistent. No matter how many miracles they saw, the people often reverted to doubt at the first sign of hardship. Spies sent to scout the Promised Land returned with glowing descriptions of milk and honey, but also terrifying tales of giants and fortified cities. The people's courage collapsed, and they refused to enter. The consequence was brutal, forty years of wandering until that doubting generation had passed away.

So the wilderness years stretch on, both bleak and formative. There were rebellions, Korah and his followers challenging Moses' leadership, Miriam and Aaron questioning his authority. There were moments of astonishing provision and moments of equally astonishing pettiness. There were deaths, Miriam and Aaron themselves, and later Moses, who glimpsed the Promised Land but did not enter.

It is hard not recognise something deeply human, the tendency to forget gratitude, the lure of the familiar even when the familiar was oppressive, the difficulty of trusting in promises that seem perpetually postponed. And yet, in this strange desert classroom, a people were shaped. They were no longer just a mass of ex-slaves. They became a community with laws, worship, leaders, and a story to tell their children, a story of survival in a place where survival should not have been possible.

By the time they reached the Jordan River, poised to cross into the land at last, they were a different people than the frightened, bewildered crowd that had staggered out of Egypt. The desert had burned away illusions, tested their loyalties, and given them an identity. It was not a pleasant process, but it was unforgettable.

Chapter Fourteen - Joshua and the Promised Land

After forty years of wandering, the Israelites finally stood on the brink of Canaan, the land promised to Abraham, Isaac, and Jacob. For decades, their lives had been a mixture of miracles, complaints, and survival lessons in a desert that did not negotiate. Now, the mountains and rivers of the promised territory lay ahead, a patchwork of fertile valleys, fortified towns, and, from their reports, giants that made the older generation's knees quake.

Joshua, formerly a spy among the twelve scouts, now assumed leadership. He was a man seasoned not just by desert life but by experience with both success and failure. Moses, who had guided the people through miracles and calamities, had trained him well, passing on not only the law and strategy but the patient endurance necessary to lead a stubborn, sometimes absurdly ungrateful population.

Crossing the Jordan River was itself a spectacle. The river, swollen by seasonal rains, stopped flowing as the priests carrying the Ark of the Covenant stepped into the water. The Israelites waded across on dry ground, carrying tents, livestock, and, no doubt, the occasional lost sheep. Imagine the noise, the confusion, the delight, and the awkward scrambling of children and animals.

Once on the other side, the real challenge began, claiming a land already inhabited. Canaan was not empty, nor unprepared. It had cities, kings, armies, and walls. The first major test was Jericho, a city famous for its massive fortifications. Joshua followed God's instructions and the people marched around the walls for seven days, carrying the Ark, blowing trumpets, and, on the seventh day, shouting. The walls fell. And yes, it probably looked utterly bewildering to anyone observing from the outside, a mass of people circling walls like a prolonged, ritualistic parade, yet achieving something astonishing.

From there, conquest continued and sometimes with more strategy than spectacle, sometimes with divine intervention. Cities fell, alliances formed and dissolved, and tribes settled into territories. The Promised Land, while rich and fertile, was hardly unchallenged. This was a landscape full of hills, valleys, and human resistance, and the Israelites learned to navigate both.

But the story of Canaan is as much about organisation as warfare. Joshua divided the land among the tribes, setting boundaries, allotting cities, and making sure each group knew its inheritance. They built altars, renewed the covenant, and attempted, at last, to live by the laws and principles given at Sinai. It was a strange mix of human ingenuity, political pragmatism, and obedience to divine instruction and a messy but sincere effort to create a functioning society from a people who had spent most of their history wandering in the desert.

And there were ceremonies, important, sometimes absurd, and often joyous. Circumcision was reinstated for those born in the wilderness, festivals were celebrated, and boundaries were formally acknowledged. The people who had grumbled at manna, water, and quail were now laying down roots. They were farmers, priests, and warriors in a land that had both welcomed and resisted them.

Joshua's leadership was steady, practical, and devout. He reminded the people of their history, their covenant, and their obligations. "Choose this day whom you will serve," he said, recognising that the challenge of freedom is not just survival but discipline and fidelity. The Israelites had crossed seas, survived deserts, and defeated cities, but now they faced the subtler battles, how to live together, honour their God, and manage abundance without repeating the mistakes of the past.

The Promised Land was both the culmination of generations of promise and the start of something entirely new. It was fertile, bright, and full of possibility, but also contested, and demanding of courage, wisdom, and patience. Joshua's success lay not only in conquest but in shaping the Israelites into a people capable of remembering their history, obeying their laws, and living in covenant with God.

In many ways, the land itself became a teacher, much like the wilderness had been. It demanded effort, strategy, respect, and care. And after all the wandering, the trials, and the miraculous interventions, the Israelites were finally in a place where their story could settle, grow, and multiply, a living testament to generations of endurance, faith, and occasional bewildering absurdity.

Chapter Fifteen - The Judges and cycles of rebellion

If the Exodus, the wilderness wanderings, and the conquest of Canaan were the story of a people learning to walk, the period of the Judges is the story of them learning to stand upright, wobble, and occasionally trip over their own feet, again and again. Imagine a patchwork of tribes scattered across the rolling hills, fertile valleys, and arid plains of Canaan, each trying to maintain some sense of order, each dealing with neighbours who were just as determined to hang onto their territory.

There was no centralised government, no king, no permanent military or bureaucracy. Instead, the Israelites were governed by a loose confederation, often rallying under leaders called Judges, who were not judges in the modern sense but charismatic deliverers and warriors raised up in times of crisis. And crisis, as it turned out, was a constant companion.

The cycle was remarkably predictable, almost comically so if you step back. First, the people would grow complacent. Peace and prosperity would settle over the land, and the Israelites, having tasted freedom, would often forget the God who had delivered them. Idolatry, assimilation, and general neglect of the covenant would creep in. Sometimes, they would turn to Baal or other local gods, sometimes they would just lapse into a kind of chaotic self-interest, squabbling among themselves.

Then, as if on cue, a neighbouring people, Philistines, Moabites, Midianites, or Canaanites would take advantage of the slackened vigilance. Tribes were raided, cities were pillaged, and oppression returned. The people, predictably, panicked and cried out. It's a bit like a seasonal storm hitting a village that refuses to maintain its dikes, disaster arrives, then complaints, then a desperate search for rescue.

At this point, God would raise up a Judge. And these were fascinating characters, full of human quirks and remarkable abilities. Othniel was the first, a relatively obscure figure who nevertheless delivered his people when the Moabites pressed in. Ehud was left-handed, a fact that turns out to be crucial in his assassination of a king and demonstrates that sometimes the divine plan appreciates a bit of human idiosyncrasy. Deborah, a prophetess and military leader, combined wisdom with decisiveness, commanding armies from under a palm tree while her general, Barak, followed her orders. Imagine her consulting battle plans with a sense of practicality and flair.

And then there's Gideon, the man of modest beginnings, threshing wheat in secret to avoid the Midianites, who would later lead an army of three hundred men. Triumph was miraculous, not logistical. Armed not with swords but with torches hidden inside clay jars, trumpets, and faith, they launched a night-time attack. When Gideon's men broke the jars to reveal the torches and blew their trumpets, shouting "A sword for the Lord and for Gideon!" The Midianite camp was thrown into chaos. Believing they were surrounded by a huge force, the enemy soldiers turned on each other and fled. If there were ever a war manual titled *How to Win by Confusing Everyone*, this episode would top the list.

Jephthah, the exile-turned-commander, is another study in human complexity. He was brave and shrewd, but tragically impulsive. His story includes an oath that leads to heart-wrenching consequences, reminding us that even divinely appointed leaders are flawed humans, capable of terrible errors despite noble intentions.

Jephthah was an outcast from his own family. His father, Gilead, had other sons by a different wife, and Jephthah's mother was not part of the main family line, so he was effectively disowned. He grew up on the fringes, gathering a band of "lawless men" around him, a rough, independent group who probably had no illusions about life's fairness.

When the Ammonites threatened Gilead, the elders of the tribe came to Jephthah and asked him to lead them, promising that he would become their head if he succeeded. This reluctant leader accepted, but first he tried diplomacy, he sent envoys to the Ammonite king, arguing that the Israelites had not wronged them and that the territory dispute was actually the Ammonites' misunderstanding. The king refused, and war became inevitable.

Here's where the story becomes grim and unforgettable. Before battle, Jephthah made a rash vow to God, if he was given victory over the Ammonites, he would offer as a sacrifice whatever came out of his house to greet him when he returned. Jephthah then led the Israelites to a decisive military victory.

Tragically, when he returned home, the first person to come out of his house was his only daughter, dancing to celebrate his triumph. The story says he was devastated, but bound by the vow he had made. He fulfilled the vow, she was sacrificed. It's a story that lingers with sorrow, showing the consequences of impulsive promises and human misjudgement, even in the context of heroic leadership.

Jephthah's story is a cautionary tale layered over a heroic narrative, a man who rose from outcast status to save his people, yet whose own choices brought terrible personal cost. Even divinely appointed leaders are fallible, impulsive, and subject to tragedy.

The cycle continued endlessly. Peace, prosperity, forgetfulness, oppression, repentance, deliverance, peace again. There was Samson, whose strength was legendary, his flaws just as legendary, and whose stories border on slapstick, fighting lions with his bare hands, toppling pillars, and yet constantly being undone by personal weaknesses and entanglements with Philistine women.

Through it all, the Israelites' life was messy, unpredictable, sometimes heroic, and sometimes foolish. The Judges themselves were not kings, not bureaucrats, not central authorities, they were episodic sparks of leadership, called up in moments of crisis, and then fading back into the background once the immediate threat was vanquished. Leadership was temporary, covenantal fidelity was fragile and human nature remained delightfully, disastrously consistent.

In some ways, the wilderness lessons persisted in the Promised Land. The Israelites could claim territory and live in abundance, yet they were still learning the hard lesson that freedom requires discipline, vigilance, and humility. The covenant from Sinai was never a one-off ceremony. It had to be lived daily, remembered constantly, and enacted in both devotion and practical behaviour. And time after time, the people discovered that neglecting this responsibility led to chaos, while obedience brought deliverance, even if the deliverance came wrapped in eccentric human personalities, improbable tactics, and divine surprises.

The period of the Judges, therefore, is both frustrating and fascinating. It is human history at its rawest, a mixture of courage and cowardice, wisdom and folly, faith and forgetfulness. It is a patchwork of victories and defeats,

81

stories of unlikely heroes and near-catastrophes, and a record of a people still discovering what it meant to be a nation, not just in terms of land or power, but in terms of identity, purpose, and relationship with God.

The stories of the Judges are episodic, dramatic, and full of detail, from Deborah's strategic genius to Gideon's night ambush, from Jephthah's tragic oath to Samson's comic violence. Together, they create a portrait of a people who are heroic, foolish, and resilient in equal measure, humans learning, painfully and spectacularly, what it means to live as God's chosen under the uncertain skies of history.

And yet, despite the chaos and repetition, there is an underlying rhythm. Sin, suffering, repentance, and deliverance repeat in a way that is almost comforting, a divine pattern that says, "Even when you fail, guidance, rescue, and new opportunity are not far away." For the Israelites, the wilderness may have ended, but the lessons of trust, vigilance, and humility continued in cycles, preparing them for the more stable, yet politically complex, era of monarchy to come.

Chapter Sixteen - Samuel, Saul, and the rise of kingship

After the tumultuous period of the Judges, Israel found itself in a peculiar position. They had survived the wilderness, conquered the Promised Land, and endured decades of cyclical rebellion and deliverance. But survival, as anyone who has ever dealt with bureaucracies, neighbours, or toddlers knows, does not automatically translate into smooth governance. Israel's tribal structure, admirable in some ways, had limits with no central authority, constant vulnerability to external threats, and the occasional internecine squabble.

Enter Samuel, a man whose story begins with miraculous circumstances. His mother, Hannah, had long been childless and prayed fervently for a son, promising to dedicate him to God. God answered her prayers, and Samuel was born. Even as a boy, he demonstrated a remarkable sense of purpose, serving in the tabernacle under Eli, the high priest. Imagine a boy navigating the corridors of power, incense curling around him, while learning to discern voices, not just human ones, but divine ones. Samuel grew into a prophet and judge, the final link between the era of Judges and the new age of monarchy.

Now, the Israelites, practical as ever, had a problem. "A king! We want a king!" they demanded of Samuel. To Samuel, this was unsettling. God had been their king and a human monarch seemed almost a step backward. Yet God allowed it. So Israel, weary of insecurity, factional disputes, and foreign pressures, formally requested monarchy.

The first king was Saul, a man of impressive stature and presence, chosen in part because of his physical appearance and the aura of leadership he carried. Imagine a man taller than most, commanding attention, suddenly anointed by Samuel, the prophet, amid cheers, awe, and probably a good deal of confusion. Saul had charisma, bravery, and the sort of confidence that makes people follow, at least at first.

Early in his reign, Saul proved his worth. He rallied tribes, defeated the Ammonites, and demonstrated courage in battle. Israel, for a moment, felt secure. A human king was practical, decisive, and visible which was a stark contrast to the sometimes obscure, episodic leadership of the Judges.

Yet Saul's reign also illustrates a key principle of human governance which is that charisma is not enough. As threats continued and God's guidance became clear, Saul struggled with obedience and patience. He made mistakes and impulsive decisions, half-hearted executions of divine commands, and attempts to consolidate power in ways that conflicted with the principles he was meant to uphold. His failures were not catastrophic immediately, but they sowed the seeds of tension between himself, Samuel, and God.

At this point, Samuel, ever the perceptive prophet, prepares the way for David. He anoints a young shepherd from Bethlehem, not a warrior, not a political insider, but a boy with faith, courage, and unexpected wisdom. David's rise signals the beginning of a new era, one in which kingship, divine favour, human ambition, and political reality intersect in ways that will reshape Israel forever.

The transition from Judges to monarchy is remarkable. Israel, a people accustomed to episodic leadership and divine miracles, now contends with the challenges of centralized power. They now had a king who must be obeyed, an army that must be led, and a nation learning to balance freedom, obedience, and human ambition. It is messy, human, and profoundly instructive.

Even at this early stage, one can see the patterns that will recur throughout Israelite history, human pride, divine guidance, obedience and rebellion, and the inescapable intertwining of leadership and personal character. Samuel, Saul, and the rise of kingship are less about perfection than about the ongoing struggle to govern, to lead, and to remain faithful under conditions that are inherently difficult and often absurdly unpredictable.

Chapter Seventeen – David and God's covenant

God's covenant is essentially a binding agreement or relationship between God and humanity or more specifically between God and the people of Israel. The term "covenant" isn't just legalistic. It's relational, moral, spiritual, and sometimes even nationalistic. It carries promises, responsibilities, and consequences. It is a pact with both sides having roles to play, though God's part is usually faithful and generous.

God's covenant is the thread that runs through the wilderness, the judges, the monarchy, and the promises to the people. It is the backbone, sometimes followed closely, sometimes ignored, but always shaping the narrative and Israel's identity.

The covenant, first formalised at Sinai, is essentially an agreement that God promises to be Israel's God, guide them, protect them, and give them the land, while the people promise obedience, faithfulness, and moral conduct. At Sinai, this was symbolised by the Ten Commandments, the tabernacle, and ritual laws. Binding God and Israel together in mutual commitment.

During the Judges, the covenant is tested repeatedly. The people fall into idolatry or forgetfulness, cycles of rebellion emerge, and God's intervention comes through Judges. Every time the Israelites turn back to God, even briefly, the covenant activates deliverance and the framework is there, the rules are known, but human nature is messy. The covenant functions as both a safety net and a moral compass. It explains why God acts in judgement, why deliverance comes, and why the people must remember their obligations.

When Saul and David rise, the covenant takes on a new dimension. It now interacts with kingship. The monarchy isn't outside the covenant, it's meant to operate within it. David, for instance, is described as "a man after God's own heart," not because he's flawless, but because he seeks to align his kingship with God's promises. The covenant legitimises his rule, provides moral and spiritual guidance, and promises enduring favour to his lineage (the famous Davidic covenant). Saul's failures, by contrast, show that monarchy is still constrained by covenantal obedience, charisma and military prowess cannot substitute for faithfulness.

With Solomon, the covenant reaches a symbolic peak. The Temple embodies God's presence on earth, a tangible sign that the promises of Sinai are being realised in daily life and national identity. Yet even here, the covenant is a delicate balance of wisdom, wealth, and power, which must be matched with obedience and humility. The narrative constantly reminds us that covenantal blessing is conditional. Human ambition, arrogance, or forgetfulness can jeopardise the promise, but faithfulness ensures God's ongoing guidance.

In short, the covenant is the moral, spiritual, and narrative framework of Israel's history. It explains why God rescues, judges, or blesses. It provides the standards against which human behaviour is measured and it binds the people together across generations, from Moses to David and Solomon. The events, triumphs, mistakes, and miracles all gain meaning in light of this enduring, sometimes frustrating, always defining relationship between God and Israel.

David's rise is the stuff of legend, partly because it combines the improbable, the heroic, and the human in ways that almost beg for a wry smile. He begins as a shepherd, the youngest son of Jesse, tending sheep in the hills of Bethlehem. One imagines a boy familiar with solitude, responsible for animals that have no sense of strategy or diplomacy, honing skills in observation, patience, and improvisation. Skills, it turns out, perfectly suited for the dramatic twists ahead.

Anointed by Samuel in secret, David's first test comes not on the battlefield, but in the strange theatre of public attention. Enter Goliath, a Philistine giant of a man, literally towering over the soldiers of Israel. The armies freeze in terror, morale plummets, and young David steps forward armed with nothing but a sling and unshakable confidence. The story is as much psychological as physical, a boy confronting not just a giant, but the collective fear of a nation. One stone, one swing, and Goliath falls. David's improbable victory becomes a national symbol where courage, ingenuity, and faith outweigh brute force.

David's reign is not without complexity. He navigates civil wars, rival claims, betrayals, and personal failings. His leadership blends charisma, strategic acumen, and, occasionally, impulsive decision-making. David is both an inspired poet and a flawed human. He consolidates the tribes of Israel, establishes Jerusalem as the political and spiritual capital, and carries the Ark of the Covenant there, symbolically and literally centralising the nation's identity. Jerusalem becomes more than a city. It is a symbol of unity, faith, and ambition.

This is also a period of remarkable cultural and artistic flourish. David composes psalms, a body of poetry that blends praise, lament, reflection, and spiritual aspiration. These songs, rooted in personal experience and national life, give voice to the collective consciousness of Israel, a people who have wandered, fought, and struggled for identity. The psalms are enduring because they are human first, emotional, vivid, and intimately aware of both fear and hope.

David's son, Solomon, then takes the story into a new phase of peace, prosperity, and monumental ambition. Solomon's reign is marked by diplomacy, trade, and a fascination with wisdom. He constructs the Temple in Jerusalem, a structure designed to embody Israel's covenant with God. Architects, craftsmen, stonecutters, and goldsmiths all working in concert, all under the eye of a king who seems as intrigued by details of design as by theological import. The Temple is not merely a building but a statement of identity, devotion, and permanence.

Solomon is also famous for his wisdom, a mix of keen observation, practical judgement, and insight into human nature. The story of two women disputing a child's parentage captures this beautifully. He proposes dividing the child in two, revealing the true mother through her instinct to protect. It's a moment that blends legal acumen, psychological insight, and dramatic flair, precisely the qualities a king needs to navigate a complex, newly unified nation.

Yet Solomon's reign, for all its glory, carries the seeds of later difficulty. Extravagance, polygamy, and political alliances through marriage create tensions, both internally and with neighbouring nations. Even in a golden age, human ambition and desire complicate the pure ideals of governance, reminding us that prosperity and wisdom are often entwined with folly.

The era of David and Solomon is, in many ways, the story of Israel learning to be a nation in a tangible sense. From shepherds and wandering tribes, they become citizens of a centralized, organised, and ambitious kingdom. They learn to balance faith, politics, artistry, and practicality though never perfectly. Leadership, the covenant, and human character intertwine in ways that are as instructive as they are entertaining.

Through David and Solomon, we see the promise of Israel realised in visible form, the land settled, the tribes unified, the Temple built, and the psalms composed. Yet even amid triumph, the narrative never loses its wryly human perspective. Leaders are brilliant and flawed, victories are hard-won, and the lessons of obedience, humility, and vigilance are never far from the surface.

Chapter Eighteen - Solomon and the temple

The Ark of the Covenant is an iconic and mysterious object. It's essentially a sacred chest, a physical manifestation of God's presence among the Israelites, and a symbol of the covenant between God and His people. Think of it as part throne, part relic.

This Ark is made of acacia wood, overlaid with gold inside and out. It has a gold lid called the mercy seat, flanked by two cherubim with wings outstretched. It's portable, designed to be carried on poles inserted through rings attached to its sides, so that the people could transport it during their wanderings in the wilderness.

Traditionally, the Ark contained the two stone tablets of the Ten Commandments, the concrete, literal representation of the covenant. Some also suggest it held Aaron's rod and a pot of manna, though the Ten Commandments are the central focus. These items made the Ark both a sacred relic and a symbol of divine law and provision.

The Ark is not a magical object in the casual sense, it is God's presence made tangible. Wherever the Ark goes, it signifies that God is there. In battle, it serves as a rallying point and a sign of divine support. In the Tabernacle and later the Temple, it occupies the Holy of Holies, the most sacred space where only the high priest may enter once a year on Yom Kippur, symbolising a direct line to God.

The Ark is associated with several dramatic events in Israel's history. The waters of the Jordan parted when the Ark was carried across. The walls of Jericho fell after it was circled around the city. It even caused fear and defeat among Israel's enemies when mishandled, showing that it was not just a symbolic object but a vessel demanding respect and obedience.

In short, the Ark of the Covenant is a portable throne of God, a reminder that God is both transcendent and present with His people. It embodies law, covenant, and divine presence in a single, awe-inspiring object, linking the Israelites' daily life, worship, and national identity to the promises and guidance of God.

Let's shift focus back to Solomon. He ascends the throne at a moment of relative peace. The armies are secure, the tribes unified, and the kingdom's wealth growing. It's the perfect time for grand ambition, and Solomon certainly has ambition. But he isn't just thinking about palaces and riches, he's thinking about God, identity, and legacy. The crown jewel of his vision is the Temple in Jerusalem, a building intended to house the Ark of the Covenant and serve as the spiritual centre of the nation.

The scale of the project is staggering. Solomon mobilises tens of thousands of labourers, craftsmen, and specialists. Stonecutters haul massive blocks from quarries, carpenters fashion cedar beams imported from Lebanon, goldsmiths and weavers create intricate decorations. This is a construction site spanning acres, echoing with hammer strikes, the smell of cedar, dust swirling, and workers moving with precision that seems almost choreographed. It's not just a building, it's a statement. This is Israel, unified, devoted, and ambitious.

Solomon's Temple is designed with precision and symbolism. The inner sanctuary, the Holy of Holies, is where the Ark will reside, accessible only to the high priest once a year. Outside that, the main hall, courtyards, altars, and chambers create layers of sacred space, each carefully structured to reflect spiritual hierarchy and divine presence. Even the decorative motifs, cherubim, palm trees, and open flowers, carry theological meaning. Nothing is accidental. The Temple is theology made tangible, a blueprint of devotion in stone, wood, and gold.

The dedication ceremony itself is dramatic. Solomon stands before the assembly of Israelites, raising his hands in prayer. Smoke curls from sacrifices, a cloud of incense fills the air, and God's presence is said to descend, filling the Temple in a way that makes the assembled worshippers tremble. Imagine the awe. Decades of wandering, conquest, and leadership condensed into a single moment of tangible, overwhelming holiness. It is spiritual architecture at its most ambitious, merging human craftsmanship and divine inspiration.

Yet Solomon's story is never purely about triumph. His wisdom, which attracts dignitaries like the Queen of Sheba, also comes with a heavy dose of human complexity. He maintains political alliances through marriage, amasses wealth on a scale almost comically large for a desert nation, and builds a kingdom whose prosperity relies on taxation and forced labour. There is genius here, but also hubris, a reminder that even in the golden age, human ambition and divine favour exist in a delicate balance.

Solomon's Temple, though eventually destroyed centuries later, becomes the enduring symbol of Israel's covenantal relationship with God. It is the physical manifestation of promises first made to Abraham, formalised at Sinai, and carried forward through David's reign. The Temple embodies identity, faith, and the hope that God's presence can dwell among a people who have struggled, wandered, and persevered.

In short, Solomon's Temple is more than architecture, it is poetry, politics, and theology intertwined. It represents the height of human aspiration within the framework of divine covenant. This is a people's devotion made manifest, their history crystallised.

Chapter Nineteen - Division of the kingdom

Solomon's reign, for all its splendour and wisdom, contained seeds of instability. His ambitious building projects, extravagant wealth, and political alliances through multiple marriages weighed heavily on the people. Taxes and forced labour bred discontent among the northern tribes, whose memory of the wilderness and tribal autonomy made them sensitive to heavy-handed central authority. By the time Solomon died, the stage was set for division.

Enter Rehoboam, Solomon's son. He inherits the throne, young and perhaps inexperienced, yet full of royal entitlement. When the northern tribes come to him with a simple request to lighten the burdens imposed by his father, Rehoboam asks for advice. The elders suggest compromise and patience, but his peers counsel him to assert authority ruthlessly. Rehoboam chooses the latter, declaring, "My little finger shall be thicker than my father's loins!" In essence, it was an ancient way of saying, "You think my father was tough? I'm far tougher." The northern tribes, predictably, rebel.

Thus, the kingdom splits. Ten tribes form Israel under the leadership of Jeroboam, a former official under Solomon who had fled to Egypt before returning as a political saviour.

Judah and Benjamin remain loyal to Rehoboam, forming Judah in the south, centred on Jerusalem and the Temple. This division, though politically practical, fractures the nation spiritually, culturally, and economically.

The new northern kingdom of Israel quickly establishes rival religious centres to consolidate power. Jeroboam erects golden calves at Bethel and Dan, ostensibly to provide the northern tribes with local worship sites rather than forcing pilgrimages to Jerusalem. This is a brilliant political move, though fraught theologically. The calves are meant to prevent rebellion, yet they also spark cycles of idolatry that prophets will later condemn relentlessly.

Judah, in contrast, retains the Temple in Jerusalem and the Davidic dynasty, but it too is not immune from sin and disobedience. Kings rise and fall, some devout, others corrupt. Both kingdoms wrestle with the same tension of maintaining loyalty to God while navigating the messiness of human ambition, family rivalry, and foreign threats.

Foreign powers loom large in this period. Egypt, Assyria, and later Babylon interfere regularly, exploiting internal divisions. Alliances are made and broken with alarming frequency, and prophets emerge as both moral guides and alarmists, warning the people that abandoning the covenant will bring disaster. Elijah and Elisha, for example, confront kings and challenge widespread idol worship, demonstrating that faithfulness is rarely convenient or popular.

The cycle that characterised the Judges continues in a new form. Kings rise, the people prosper, and then rebellion and idolatry follow. God, through prophets, warns, judges, and occasionally offers reprieve. The narrative becomes a tapestry of political intrigue, military campaigns, religious fidelity and failure, and human character in all its glory and folly.

In essence, the division of the kingdom transforms Israelite history from a single, ambitious monarchy into a complex, dual-nation. The covenant, the Temple, and the Ark continue to shape identity, but the practical realities of politics, geography, and human weakness complicate obedience. Each kingdom navigates its own challenges, yet both are bound to the covenant.

The divided kingdom sets the stage for cycles of prosperity, idolatry, prophetic warning, conquest, and exile, a pattern that will dominate Israelite history for centuries to come, offering lessons on leadership, faith, and human folly that remain startlingly relevant.

Chapter Twenty - Prophets and the call to repentance

The divided kingdoms of Israel and Judah are like two siblings who cannot agree on anything, one constantly looking over its shoulder at the other, both simultaneously defiant and fragile. Israel in the north, with its ten tribes, is politically ambitious but spiritually erratic. Jeroboam's golden calves, meant to consolidate loyalty, become a template for centuries of idolatry. Meanwhile, Judah in the south, anchored by Jerusalem and the Davidic line, struggles to remain faithful, even while enjoying relative stability.

Into this turbulent landscape step the prophets, figures as bold and sometimes exasperating as any modern whistle-blower. They are the voices crying in the wilderness, insisting that faithfulness to God's covenant matters above convenience, political expedience, or ritual formality. They warn, they chastise, they foretell, and they often do so at personal risk.

Take Elijah, for example. Operating in the northern kingdom during the reign of Ahab and the notorious Queen Jezebel, he confronts idolatry head-on. The story of the contest on Mount Carmel is legendary. Elijah challenges hundreds of prophets of Baal to demonstrate whose god is real. The prophets dance, shout, and even injure themselves in a desperate ritual, but nothing happens. Then Elijah prays, and fire descends from heaven to consume the sacrifice. It is spectacular, theatrical, and terrifying, a vivid illustration that God's presence is active, real, and demanding of attention.

Elijah's successor, Elisha, continues the work, performing miracles, advising kings, and intervening in battles. Together, these prophets act as moral navigators, attempting to steer a people whose political and religious life is frequently chaotic, opportunistic, and distracted. Their work is rarely appreciated in the moment, but history records them as vital witnesses to both divine justice and mercy.

Despite prophetic warnings, the northern kingdom of Israel struggles to remain faithful. Assyria, a rising imperial power, watches carefully and eventually intervenes. By the mid-8th century BC, internal corruption, idolatry, and political instability leave Israel vulnerable. Prophets like Hosea deliver stark messages, often couched in metaphor. Israel is an unfaithful spouse, a nation that forgets its obligations, flirting with foreign gods while ignoring the God who delivered it. Ultimately, the warnings go unheeded, and around 722 BC, Assyria conquers Israel, scattering the ten tribes and ending the northern kingdom as a political entity. The exile is both punishment and consequence, illustrating the practical risks of political and spiritual failure.

Judah, while somewhat more stable, is not immune. Kings rise and fall. Prophets such as Isaiah, Micah, and later

Jeremiah deliver repeated warnings. Wealth, military alliances, and ostentation cannot substitute for obedience and humility. Judah experiences cycles of reform and relapse, briefly flourishing under kings like Hezekiah and Josiah, who attempt to restore covenantal fidelity, purify worship, and centralise religious practice. But prosperity and pride often breed complacency, and foreign powers, Babylon in particular, become an existential threat.

By the late 7th and early 6th centuries BC, prophecy meets reality in the Babylonian exile. Jerusalem falls, the Temple is destroyed, and much of the population is deported. It is a devastating moment. The political centre, the sacred heart of worship, and the cultural hub are all upended. The Ark's earlier symbolic role, once the tangible presence of God, becomes a poignant memory. Even the Temple itself, the pinnacle of Solomon's architectural ambition, is razed.

Yet the covenant persists. Even in exile, prophets offer hope, insisting that the relationship between God and Israel is not broken. Ezekiel, in vivid and sometimes surreal visions, promises restoration, a renewal of life and law, and eventual return to the land. Second Isaiah, writing to a people in captivity, emphasises redemption, justice, and God's enduring faithfulness. The covenant, though tested, becomes the framework through which despair is transformed into hope, exile into expectation, and loss into the promise of return.

This era, with its prophets, political intrigue, and exiles, demonstrates the dual nature of the covenant. It is at once moral and practical, spiritual and political. Obedience and faithfulness bring guidance and blessing. Rebellion and neglect bring vulnerability and consequence. Human ambition, folly, and courage all play out within this framework, giving the narrative both grandeur and intimacy.

In short, the period of the divided kingdom, prophetic intervention, and exile is a study in contrasts. Faithfulness and failure, political calculation and divine instruction, despair and hope. It's a story full of missteps, courage, and the perennial tension between short-term survival and long-term covenantal fidelity.

Chapter Twenty One - Exile of Israel

If you were living in the northern kingdom of Israel in the 8th century BC, you would have felt as if history itself had picked up speed. Life had once been fairly straightforward with villages and farms clinging to hillsides, local shrines humming with sacrifices, kings rising and falling in Jerusalem and Samaria, prophets occasionally showing up to shout warnings. But by the time Assyria began flexing its imperial muscles, the world suddenly seemed much bigger, scarier, and far less under control.

Assyria, for context, was not the sort of empire you wanted as a neighbour. These were people who had perfected the art of conquest, not only through military might but through psychological warfare. They carved reliefs showing themselves impaling enemies on stakes and deporting whole populations, and then they displayed those reliefs proudly on palace walls. Their message was simple, if you resist, then you will be obliterated, if you surrender, then you might at least live to tell the tale.

The kingdom of Israel, however, did not heed the warnings. Prophet after prophet, Amos, Hosea, Isaiah (speaking partly to the north as well) all cried out that idolatry, injustice, and political entanglements with foreign powers were dragging the nation toward disaster. But kings and people alike largely ignored them. Israel chased after Baal and Asherah, cut deals with Egypt and Aram, and tried to outplay the Assyrian colossus with the diplomatic subtlety of a gambler who keeps doubling down on bad bets.

By 722 BC, the Assyrians had had enough. They swept down with terrifying efficiency, besieging the capital, Samaria. Siege warfare in the ancient world was ghastly business with walls surrounded, supplies cut off, famine setting in. Disease was spreading faster than hope. After three years of grinding pressure, Samaria fell.

What followed was as much cultural engineering as conquest. Assyria did not simply want tribute, it wanted stability. And stability, in their view, was achieved by mixing populations until no one quite remembered who they were anymore. Large swathes of Israel's population were deported to far-off regions of the empire, places like Media and Mesopotamia, while foreigners from elsewhere were transplanted into Israelite territory. Families were torn apart, languages confused, and entire communities dissolved into the vast Assyrian machine.

This policy gave rise to what later generations would call the "lost ten tribes of Israel." Unlike Judah, which would later return from Babylonian exile, the northern tribes seemed to vanish into history, absorbed by other peoples and lands. Their disappearance left a haunting echo, a kind of unfinished sentence in Israel's story.

For those left behind, life was equally disorienting. New settlers brought their gods and customs, mixing with lingering Israelite practices, creating a hybrid religion that future generations would view suspiciously. This is the seedbed of the Samaritans, who centuries later appear as both neighbours and rivals to the Jews.

Theologically, the exile was a thunderclap. It forced Israel to confront the covenant in brutally practical terms. The prophets had said that idolatry and injustice would lead to ruin, and here was the ruin, vividly real. Hosea's image of Israel as an unfaithful spouse suddenly wasn't just poetry, it was history written in ashes and displacement. Amos's thunderous warnings about social injustice like the trampling of the poor, and the selling of the needy for a pair of sandals, now sounded less like hyperbole and more like a final verdict.

And yet, even amid the devastation, hope flickered. Prophets like Hosea insisted that exile was not the end, that God's covenantal love was more stubborn than human betrayal. The land might be emptied, the people scattered, but God was not done. Exile was both punishment and opportunity. This was a stripping away of false securities, forcing the people to reckon with what it truly meant to belong to God.

The exile of Israel stands as both a historical catastrophe and a theological lesson. Politically, it was the end of the northern kingdom. Spiritually, it was a reckoning and a demonstration that covenant was not a licence for complacency but a living relationship that demanded faithfulness. The people were scattered, yes, but the story was not over. Not yet.

Chapter Twenty Two - Exile of Judah

The fall of the northern kingdom to Assyria was a loud warning, and the Exile of Judah was the climactic crash of the warning ignored. It is the moment when Jerusalem, the beating heart of Israel's faith and national identity, was torn open, its Temple reduced to ash, and its people marched into captivity. And yet, curiously, it is also the moment when Judaism as we know it today truly began to take shape.

Judah had always thought of itself as the sturdier sibling of Israel. After all, Israel in the north had collapsed in 722 BC, swallowed up by Assyria, while Judah in the south soldiered on, centred on Jerusalem and the house of David. It had the Temple, the Ark (at least for a time), and the covenant promises spoken to David, that his line would endure. Judah saw itself as the keeper of the flame. But faithfulness and national pride are not the same thing, and Judah's story, too, slid into the same weary cycle of reform, complacency, idolatry, and rebellion.

The prophets were uncomfortably clear about it. Isaiah, in his great sweeping poetry, warned Jerusalem not to place trust in military alliances. Micah thundered against corruption, reminding Judah that God wanted not ritual excess but justice, mercy, and humility. Jeremiah, later, stood in the courts of the Temple itself and declared that sacrifices and festivals meant nothing if injustice thrived in the streets.

These men weren't critics of faith but rather they were critics of empty faith, of religion without heart. But, like the prophets of the north before them, they were rarely thanked for it.

By the late 7th century BC, Judah found itself caught between two rising superpowers. Egypt was to the southwest and Babylon to the northeast. Assyria had faded, but Babylon was ascendant. Kings of Judah tried to navigate this delicate balance, sometimes leaning toward Egypt, sometimes bending the knee to Babylon. It was, at best, precarious, at worst, suicidal.

The tipping point came under King Zedekiah, who thought it wise to rebel against Babylonian control. It was not wise. In 586 BC, the Babylonians, led by King Nebuchadnezzar II, descended on Judah. Jerusalem was besieged, and if you can imagine being inside a city under siege in the ancient world, it was nothing short of hell. Food dwindled, disease spread, walls trembled under battering rams, and despair set in. After months of this slow death, the Babylonians broke through.

The devastation was total. The walls of Jerusalem were torn down. The Temple, the great house Solomon had built, was looted and burned. Sacred vessels were carted off to Babylon. The Davidic palace crumbled. Zedekiah, the last king of Judah, tried to escape by night but was caught. In one of the more brutal moments of history, his sons were executed before his eyes, and then his eyes were put out, leaving him blind and broken, carried away to Babylon.

The people, too, were carried off, thousands deported to Babylon, others fleeing into Egypt, some left behind in the ruins. It was the end of Judah as a functioning kingdom, the end of its monarchy, and the end, at least for a time, of Jerusalem as a religious and political centre.

And yet here's the strange thing. The exile didn't kill Judah's identity. If anything, it sharpened it. In Babylon, the Judeans (from which we get the word "Jews") could no longer rely on land, king, or Temple. What they still had was the covenant, the Torah, and the stories of God's faithfulness. Synagogues began to emerge as centres of study and worship, portable faith communities untethered from a single sacred building. The exile forced them to realise that God wasn't locked in Jerusalem or confined to stone walls. He was with them even in a foreign land.

The prophets adapted to this moment too. Ezekiel, with his astonishing visions of wheels within wheels and dry bones rising to life, spoke of God's glory departing the Temple, but also of renewal, restoration, and return. Second Isaiah sang of comfort, of a highway through the wilderness, of a God who still called Israel by name. Even in Babylon, they dared to believe that exile was not the last word.

Historically, the exile of Judah created something the northern exile hadn't. A people who could be scattered and yet remain themselves. The Jews in Babylon learned how to live as a minority, distinct yet present, faithful yet adaptive. It's the seed of the Jewish diaspora, the reason why centuries later Jews could still be found in Persia, Greece, Rome, and eventually, across the world.

So the exile of Judah was both catastrophe and chrysalis. This was a catastrophe because it shattered the visible symbols of their world, symbols like their kingdom, Temple, king, and land, and a chrysalis because it transformed their faith into something portable, resilient, and enduring. When the Persian king Cyrus eventually conquered Babylon and allowed them to return, they came back not just as survivors but as a people with a stronger, more defined identity.

In short, Judah lost everything, and in that loss discovered that the covenant was not tied to walls or kings but to the living God, who could not be conquered or exiled.

Chapter Twenty Three - Return from Babylon

Before we dive straight into the return of exiled Judeans, let's explore how the Torah fits into what we see today in the modern Bible.

If you were to wander into a Christian bookstore, or for that matter, a library or an online Bible app, you'd quickly notice that the Bible is not just a book. It's more like a sprawling anthology written over centuries, with different authors, genres, and agendas all jammed together in a way that somehow works, like a very complicated family reunion. And at the very beginning of that reunion sits the Torah.

In the Christian Bible, the Torah corresponds to the first five books of the Old Testament: Genesis, Exodus, Leviticus, Numbers, and Deuteronomy. Five books that are, frankly, astonishing in scope. Genesis starts with the creation of the universe, which is a tricky opening, because it sets the stage for literally everything that follows, then careens through stories of humans who, if we're honest, have more in common with dramatic reality TV contestants than saintly patriarchs. Abraham barges onto the scene, Sarah argues, Isaac exists, Jacob schemes, Joseph sells his brothers down the river, and all of this establishes the groundwork for the people who will one day become Israel.

Exodus, meanwhile, is basically ancient Israel's adventure blockbuster. Moses, the reluctant hero, a burning bush, a stubborn Pharaoh, plagues, chariots, parting seas, it has everything but popcorn. And it's not just entertainment. It's about identity and who Israel is, what it means to belong to God, and what kind of society they should try (often spectacularly unsuccessfully) to build. Leviticus and Numbers then take up the less glamorous but no less crucial role of establishing rules, rituals, and social structures. It's the part that makes you think, "Ah yes, somebody had to write the instruction manual." Deuteronomy closes the set with speeches, reminders, and ethical principles that act as a kind of literary scaffolding, preparing the Israelites and us, centuries later, for the prophets who will shout, warn, and admonish with relish.

The Torah is more than historical storytelling. It's a moral and spiritual framework, like the spine of a body that supports everything else. Every prophet who thunders against injustice, every psalm that celebrates or laments, and every story of kings and exiles, all reference this spine. Even the New Testament, which Christians often think of as the crescendo of the biblical symphony, is deeply indebted to the Torah. Jesus, according to the Gospels, quotes it, interprets it, and builds on it. He doesn't treat it as quaint history. He treats it as living, breathing guidance.

Put simply, the Torah is the Bible's foundational narrative, the original script that all later chapters riff upon. Creation, humanity, the patriarchs, the Exodus, the giving of the Law, the shaping of Israel as a covenant people, these stories are like the gravitational pull around which the rest of the biblical universe orbits. Without the Torah, the prophets, psalms, historical books, and New Testament teachings would float free, beautiful perhaps, but lacking context, shape, and connection.

And here's the really fascinating thing, even though it's ancient, written thousands of years ago in a different culture and language, the Torah remains endlessly interpretable. Scholars, theologians, and curious readers can return to Genesis or Deuteronomy again and again and find new insight, new moral puzzles, and new stories that still resonate. It's a book, a set of laws, a story, and a conversation starter all in one. That's a remarkable achievement for something written in a time when most people were just trying to keep their flocks alive and figure out which way the Nile flowed.

In other words, the Torah is not just the start of the Bible but rather the blueprint, the reference point, the literary and moral North Star that makes sense of everything that follows. And like any good north star, it may feel distant at times, but it quietly guides the rest of the journey, from the psalms of joy and lament to the prophetic calls to justice, all the way to the teachings that echo into the Christian New Testament.

Now let's go back to 539 BC, when things reshuffled again. Babylon, once the great terror of the Near East, was toppled by the Persians under Cyrus the Great. Where Babylon had ruled with a heavy hand, destroying temples, scattering peoples, making subjects into trophies, Cyrus had a different approach. He saw stability not in obliteration but in restoration. His policy was to let conquered peoples return to their homelands and rebuild their shrines, provided they remained loyal and paid their dues.

For the exiled Judeans in Babylon, this was astonishing news. Imagine living for decades in a foreign land, raising children who had never seen Jerusalem, wondering if the stories of David and Solomon were just bedtime tales, and then suddenly, permission arrives from the emperor himself to go home, rebuild your Temple, and resume your worship. It must have felt like a dream

So, groups of exiles set out on the long trek westward, back to a land many of them only knew through their parents' or grandparents' stories. They came under the leadership of figures like Zerubbabel (a descendant of David) and Joshua the high priest. They trudged across the deserts, past the ruins of old Mesopotamian cities, carrying their children and what possessions they could muster, hearts full of hope and trepidation.

But the reality that awaited them was far from the golden memory. Jerusalem was a ruin, a husk of its former self. The

Temple was gone, its stones charred and toppled. Fields lay fallow, houses collapsed. Those who had remained behind including poor farmers, refugees, and foreigners resettled by Babylon were suspicious of the returning exiles. Who were these city people from Babylon, strutting in with grand talk of rebuilding, as though the land had been waiting just for them?

Still, the returnees pressed on. The first priority was the Temple. Without it, life felt incomplete. They began with an altar, simple but functional, so sacrifices could resume. First came the laying of the Temple's foundation. And here we get a wonderfully human scene, when the foundations were set there was a great shout of joy from the younger generation, excited at the prospect of a new house for God. But the older generation, those who remembered Solomon's Temple, began to weep. To them, the new foundation looked pitiful compared to the grandeur of what had been lost. Ezra records that the sound of joy and the sound of weeping blended together so that no one could tell the difference. It's one of those moments that feel painfully real, beginnings are never quite as neat as we imagine.

Work on the Temple stalled for years, plagued by local opposition and the sheer enormity of the task. Prophets like Haggai and Zechariah had to rally the people, urging them not to despise the day of small things. At last, around 516 BC, the Second Temple was completed. It wasn't as lavish as

Solomon's, but it was theirs, and it stood as a symbol that God's presence still dwelt among them.

But rebuilding walls and altars was only half the task. The greater challenge was rebuilding identity. This is where figures like Ezra and Nehemiah enter. Ezra, a scribe and priest, returned from Babylon with a passion for the Torah. He gathered the people, read the law aloud for hours, and reminded them of who they were. Not just survivors, but a covenant people. Nehemiah, a cupbearer to the Persian king, returned to rebuild the physical walls of Jerusalem, rallying people with trowel in one hand and sword in the other. Together, they gave the returnees a sense of order, purpose, and boundary.

The return was not without tension. Intermarriage with surrounding peoples sparked debates about identity. Should the returning Jews separate entirely, keeping bloodlines and practices pure, or should they find ways to integrate? Ezra took the hard line, urging strict separation. Others found this painful, even divisive. The question of what it meant to be Israel, ethnically, spiritually, culturally was as alive then as it is today.

What's striking is how the exile and return redefined Judaism. Before, the Temple and monarchy were the centrepieces. After the exile, it was the Torah which was read, studied, interpreted, that became the lifeblood of the community. Synagogues blossomed as local centres of learning and worship. Identity became less about political sovereignty and more about covenantal practice, Sabbath-keeping, dietary laws, festivals. These were things you could carry with you anywhere, whether in Jerusalem, Babylon, or beyond.

In many ways, the Return from Babylon was not an ending but the beginning of a new chapter, the formation of the Judaism that would survive foreign rule, exile again, and even the destruction of the Second Temple centuries later. It gave the people a resilience that empire after empire could not extinguish.

So, the return was messy, incomplete, and even bittersweet. But it was also a triumph of persistence, a reminder that while stones and thrones may fall, a covenant rooted in memory and practice can carry a people through anything.

Chapter Twenty Four - Waiting for the Messiah

If you were a Jew in Jerusalem, or even in Babylon or Persia, a century or two after Ezra and Nehemiah, life had a curious mix of stability and unease. The Second Temple stood modestly but sturdily, the city walls had been rebuilt, and the people had re-established a rhythm of prayer, festivals, and law. On the surface, everything might have seemed fine. But underneath, there was a simmering, almost palpable expectation that the Messiah was coming.

The word "Messiah" comes from the Hebrew mashiach, meaning "anointed one." In practice, this was a person, sometimes envisioned as a king, sometimes as a prophet, who would restore Israel, deliver justice, and bring about God's ultimate plan. Imagine telling that to people who had seen kingdoms fall, temples burned, and entire populations exiled. It was both tantalising and frustrating. Everyone wanted it to happen, but no one knew exactly when or how.

Prophets past and present had provided hints and promises. Isaiah had painted pictures of a child born to bring peace, of a figure who would shepherd the people with justice. Micah had promised a ruler from Bethlehem. Jeremiah, whose prophecies had survived exile, whispered of a "righteous Branch" from David's line who would set things right. For centuries, these prophecies hung in the air, something people could feel more than see.

But living in expectation is an oddly uncomfortable state. The daily reality of life had to continue, fields had to be tilled, taxes paid, festivals observed. And yet, in every shadow of Jerusalem's walls, in every reading of the Torah, in every whispered prayer along the River Chebar or the streets of the city, people remembered the promises. They told stories of the patriarchs, of kings, of exiles, and of God's covenant. These were not just bedtime tales. They were reminders that history was moving toward a purpose, even if it was invisible.

It wasn't just hope either, it was an anxious hope. Over the centuries, many false Messiahs arose, charismatic leaders who promised liberation, often from oppressive empires like the Seleucids or later the Romans. Some were well-meaning and others more deluded. And sometimes, as we know from history, people rallied around them only to see disaster strike. Every failed Messiah added both disappointment and a sharper edge to the expectation and the next one would have to be truly remarkable.

Life in this era, especially under foreign rule, was a balancing act. The Persian Empire gave way to the Greek Seleucids, who brought Hellenistic culture, philosophy, and sometimes aggressive policies aimed at assimilation. Then the Romans arrived, and their governance was efficient, brutal, and occasionally bewildering. For Jews living under these regimes, the dream of the Messiah was intertwined with very practical concerns, could a Davidic ruler restore autonomy, defend against oppression, and bring justice to a fractured society?

Religious thought evolved during this time. The Torah remained central, but interpretation deepened. Festivals were observed with heightened meaning. Synagogues became hubs of learning, reflection, and community cohesion. Rabbis and scribes debated, wrote, and compiled texts that would eventually form the Talmud which expands on the Torah by exploring how to apply its laws, principles, and ethical teachings in real life. Every ritual, every reading, every act of devotion became a way to stay spiritually alert, like keeping one eye on the horizon for a ship that might or might not appear.

And then there was the poetry of longing, particularly in psalms, laments, and prophetic writings. The people imagined the Messiah in multiple roles, as judge, warrior, healer, shepherd, and teacher. Each generation reshaped the expectation in response to the challenges of their time. Some imagined a political liberator who would expel oppressors while others imagined a spiritual figure that would purify the people and the Temple. The imagination ran wild, because hope, after centuries of exile, required it.

For centuries, therefore, the Jewish people lived in this strange tension that was rooted in law, ritual, and city walls rebuilt from ruin, yet perpetually looking forward. It was an expectation that shaped their identity more than almost anything else. Waiting became part of daily life, woven into stories, prayers, festivals, and teachings. It was inspiring and exhausting, a tension that would eventually prepare the ground for someone entirely unexpected, someone who would arrive not as a conquering king, but as a teacher, healer, and fulfiller of long-standing hopes.

In short, this was an era defined by anticipation. Not every day felt special, not every ruler was righteous, and not every promise seemed imminent. Yet through it all, the covenant, the Torah, the Temple, and the stories of the patriarchs and kings reminded the people that history was not random. Every exile, every return, every rebuilding, and every hardship was part of a grand design. And so the Jewish people waited, with patience, anxiety, devotion, and a sense of curiosity that would soon meet its profound moment in ways they could scarcely imagine.

Chapter Twenty Five - Birth of Jesus

Jerusalem had its Temple, modest but functional, walls rebuilt, priests performing their duties, and scribes reading the Torah aloud with ritual precision. The countryside stretched out in olive groves, vineyards, and small villages, dusty roads winding between stone houses.

The Jewish people had been waiting for centuries. They had endured exile, return, Hellenistic rule, and Roman occupation. Prophets had promised a Messiah, a Davidic heir, a righteous deliverer.

Into this world comes Mary, a young woman from the town of Nazareth, a place so modest and tucked away that most travellers barely gave it a glance. And yet, it would become iconic. Mary's life was typical for a Jewish girl of her age, betrothed to Joseph, living in a household that struggled with the practicalities of village life, keeping faith and family intertwined in everyday routines.

Then, an angel appeared. Gabriel. And Gabriel's message was unlike any routine announcement. The message was that Mary would conceive a child by the Holy Spirit, a child destined for greatness, to be called Jesus. For Mary, this was bewildering, astonishing, and terrifying in equal measure. Human imagination struggles to grasp this moment. A young girl fetching water, tending her household, suddenly confronted with huge significance.

Joseph, too, was caught in this drama. Betrothed but not yet married, he faced social, legal, and personal challenges. In a world governed by strict customs, an unplanned pregnancy could have serious repercussions. And yet, he, too, received guidance in a dream. Take Mary as your wife, care for the child, for this is part of a plan that stretches far beyond human comprehension.

Meanwhile, the Roman Empire, with its sprawling bureaucracy, edicts, and taxes, intruded even into this personal story. Caesar Augustus decreed a census, requiring Joseph and Mary to travel to Bethlehem, the city of David, because Joseph was of Davidic lineage. The journey was arduous, with rough roads, unpredictable weather, and a heavily pregnant Mary on a donkey or perhaps sometimes walking. The roads themselves had seen armies, merchants, and pilgrims for generations, but now carried this young couple on a journey that would etch them into history.

Bethlehem itself was crowded, bustling with travellers who had arrived for the census. Inns were full. Rooms were unavailable. They find a stable, a simple shelter with animals where Mary gives birth. The baby is laid not in a crib of gold or silk, but in a manger, a feeding trough for animals.

Outside, shepherds in the fields tend their flocks under a sky so wide and empty that it seems to echo eternity. Angels appear to them, proclaiming the good news. The Messiah has been born, a Saviour, bringing hope, peace, and joy. For the shepherds, common folk accustomed to long nights, watchful eyes, and the unpredictability of nature, this revelation is both terrifying and exhilarating. They hurry to see the child, carrying awe and wonder across the hillsides, speaking in breathless, imperfect sentences about what they had witnessed.

And then, there are the magi, the wise men from the East, following a star, bringing gifts of gold, frankincense, and myrrh. Their journey is long and arduous, across deserts and mountains, guided by celestial signs, their minds preoccupied with prophecy and astronomy alike. They arrive in awe, paying homage to a child whose significance the world has yet to fully comprehend.

The birth of Jesus is a moment where history, prophecy, and human experience converge, a young woman giving birth in a dusty village, a carpenter tasked with protecting and guiding the child, shepherds and wise men drawn to wonder. It is messy, humble, and yet unmistakably monumental.

And for the Jewish people who had waited for centuries, it was a moment of trembling anticipation. Could this be the Messiah? Was this the culmination of generations of hope, law, exile, and return? Only time would tell.

The birth of Jesus is not just an event, it is a beginning. A beginning that will ripple through the lives of those who witness it, through the teachings that follow, and through history itself, changing the world in ways unimaginable.

Jesus was born in Judea, a land of contrasts with dusty hills and fertile valleys, shepherds' flocks roaming alongside olive groves, Roman soldiers on patrol beside bustling marketplaces. Families raised children, farmers tended fields, craftsmen shaped wood and stone, but the undercurrent of expectation, of prophecy, gave the land a peculiar feeling. People sensed that history was alive and moving, though they could rarely predict the direction.

Mary and Joseph returned to Nazareth, their little family trying to settle into the rhythms of village life. Joseph, a carpenter, spent his days shaping wood for roofs, carts, and tables. The trade was practical, modest, and honest, and yet it provided a steady life for a young family. Mary, ever watchful, tended the household, prepared food, and guided their child in early learning. You can imagine her days full of the smells of baking bread, the warmth of a hearth, the calls of neighbours and children drifting across narrow streets.

Jesus grew in this small, unassuming town, and like any child, he learned by observation, by trial, by asking questions that sometimes exasperated adults. There were lessons in humility, in patience, in the quiet joys and frustrations. He would have observed the rhythm of the seasons, the planting

125

and harvest of fields, the flow of water in local streams. He would have listened to the elders read the Torah in the synagogue, memorising stories of creation, exile, and covenant, absorbing the poetry, law, and history that shaped his people.

Education at the time was less formal than we have today. Boys learned a trade from their fathers, memorised scripture in the synagogue, and absorbed community wisdom through stories and everyday experience. Jesus would have grown familiar with the narrative arcs of Abraham, Moses, and David, not as distant figures but as living guides shaping identity and moral imagination. There would have been festivals, Passover with its rituals and symbolic meals, Sukkot with its temporary shelters, and Shabbat with its rhythm of rest and reflection.

Life, however, was not idyllic. Judea was under Roman rule, and imperial authority could be oppressive. Taxes were collected meticulously, soldiers patrolled roads and towns, and occasional unrest reminded villagers that the world was larger and sometimes harsher than their narrow streets. Yet it is in this constrained world, that people are shaped. Observing injustice, noticing human frailty, and witnessing the tension between humility and authority, Jesus' understanding of life, ethics, and community began to take form.

Stories of miracles and signs, often associated with prophets of old, may have reached the young boy. Tales of Moses parting the sea, Elijah calling fire from heaven, and the exiles returning to rebuild a broken city were part of the cultural consciousness. They were cautionary tales, instructional stories, and seeds of wonder all at once. For a boy growing up in Nazareth, these stories were the soil in which imagination and moral reflection could flourish.

Family life was central. Siblings, cousins, and extended kin formed a network of care, social interaction, and sometimes rivalry. Meals were shared, work was collaborative, and communal prayer reinforced shared values. The Torah was read aloud regularly, and even as a child, Jesus would have begun to internalise its rhythms, laws, and moral imperatives. There was learning, yes, but also reflection, noticing the small acts of kindness, the moments of tension.

Journeys beyond Nazareth were rare but formative. Pilgrimages to Jerusalem for Passover or other festivals exposed Jesus to crowds, political authority, and ritual splendour. The Temple itself, even as the Second Temple stood more modest than Solomon's, was an architectural marvel to a child, a place of awe, ritual, and communal memory. The city bustled with merchants, pilgrims, and priests, all of whom contributed to a complex social and spiritual tapestry. For a young boy, these journeys were both education and adventure.

By the time Jesus approached adolescence, he had absorbed a deep understanding of the culture, law, and expectation of his people. He understood the rhythms of worship, the significance of covenant, and the pulse of daily life under Roman rule. He was growing not only in stature but in insight, curiosity, and spiritual awareness. Every story, every conversation, every event, the helping of a neighbour, the tending of an animal, the recitation of scripture, was preparing him for what would come next.

This was a childhood of a boy learning to navigate life, to observe the injustices and beauties of the world, and to internalise a divine narrative that stretched back thousands of years. It was in these years that the threads of hope, prophecy, and human experience were woven together. Setting the stage for a public life that would capture imagination, challenge authority, and reshape the world.

As Jesus approached young adulthood, Nazareth remained the familiar backdrop of his daily life, with the sun-baked hills, olive groves, stone houses with flat roofs, and narrow streets that rattled under the passage of donkeys and carts. Yet beneath this quiet exterior, a subtle change was taking place. The boy, who had once been fascinated by the rhythms of daily labour, by the small miracles of growth in the fields, by the stories read in the synagogue, began to notice larger patterns. He saw the inconsistencies between the laws he was taught and the way people actually lived. He noticed the burdens of taxes, the occasional arrogance of

Roman officials, the weight of social inequality, and the struggles of families.

It was the kind of observation that might pass unnoticed in many children, but not in him. Jesus had inherited the deep consciousness of generations who had endured exile, oppression, and return. He carried with him, unknowingly at first, a living memory of covenant, of law, of hope that stretched back centuries. The stories of Abraham, Isaac, Jacob, Moses, and the prophets were no longer just narratives. They were questions, challenges, and lenses through which he began to interpret life.

Nazareth itself, small and often overlooked on maps even of the time, became his classroom. There was a rhythm to village life, with mornings spent helping Joseph with carpentry, afternoons watching the elders debate scripture, evenings with families praying and recounting stories of the past. Jesus was acutely aware of human nature in all its complexity. He saw humility and pride, generosity and greed, piety and hypocrisy. He observed and reflected, learning in a way that would later inform his teaching.

Travel, while rare, expanded his perspective. Pilgrimages to Jerusalem for festivals brought him into contact with crowds, ritual, and authority on a scale Nazareth could not offer. The Temple, even in its Second-Temple modesty, was breath-taking. Its architecture, the smell of incense, the chanting of priests and Levites, the gathering of pilgrims from distant towns, all of it conveyed both human devotion and a tangible sense of the divine. A young man walking those steps would have been impressed, awed, and perhaps slightly overwhelmed. In these years, Jesus' awareness of expectation deepened. Centuries of prophetic promise lingered in the collective memory of the people. They spoke of a deliverer, a Messiah, a righteous one who would restore Israel, bring justice, and renew God's covenant. He would have heard stories whispered by elders, tales of hope, surviving exile, of kings and priests failing and succeeding, of law guiding life yet never fully satisfying human need. The anticipation was almost a tangible thing, like electricity in the air before a storm.

Conversations at home and in the synagogue were formative. Debates over the Law, interpretations of scripture, discussions about justice and mercy, these were the threads weaving themselves into his understanding. Jesus learned not only the text but the spirit of it, the questions it raised, the tensions it held. He observed how people applied it unevenly, sometimes with kindness, sometimes with rigidity. It was a human world, full of paradox and nuance, and he learned to navigate it with curiosity and discernment.

Even the simple experiences of village life, helping Joseph with carpentry, observing his mother's care, engaging with neighbours, noticing the rhythms of seasons and harvests were lessons in patience, diligence, and empathy. He saw the beauty in labour, the dignity of small acts, and the way people relied on each other in a fragile yet persistent network of community. These were not grand events, but they were formative. They shaped his understanding of life as sacred, practical and transcendent.

Village life, Torah study, pilgrimage experiences, and observation of human behaviour, prepared him. There was a stirring, subtle at first, then undeniable, a sense of purpose, a calling, recognition that his life was moving toward something larger than Nazareth, larger than carpentry, larger than even the expectations of his own people. It was as if the long centuries of hope, exile, return, and covenant had been quietly leading to this moment, to this awareness.

By the time he reached maturity, Jesus was not just a young man living in a small Galilean town. He understood human nature, deeply versed in the spiritual and legal traditions of his people, aware of the social and political forces shaping life, and beginning to sense the mission that would soon unfold. Every day, every conversation, every act of care or reflection, had been preparing him for the first public acts that would mark the beginning of his ministry.

By the time Jesus reached the age where young men in Nazareth were expected to take on adult responsibility, there was a noticeable shift in his world. The village itself remained modest, the stone houses unchanged, the olive groves as familiar as ever. Yet for Jesus, nothing felt normal anymore. He had begun to see patterns in the rhythms of life, connections between behaviour, divine law, and the slow, unfolding history of his people. There was a weight to these realizations, gentle but persistent, like the pull of a tide you can't ignore.

He continued to work with Joseph, learning more about carpentry in meticulous detail, how wood bends and yields, how a plane glides across a board, how a careful measure can save hours of work later. It was hard, honest labour, and yet it was also instructive in ways that went beyond craft. Precision, patience, creativity, problem-solving, these were skills that transcended timber and nails. Jesus absorbed them, as he absorbed the quiet rhythms of life, the subtle ways in which people interact and survive, the empathy and diligence required to care for a family and a community.

Religious study remained central. The synagogue was more than a place of worship, it was a classroom, a forum for debate, a space where questions were encouraged, and answers were rarely simple. Jesus would have sat among the elders, listening to the reading of the Torah, the interpretation of laws, and the discussion of ethical dilemmas. Some of these conversations were mundane, almost pedantic while others were profound, wrestling with morality, justice, and mercy.

Travel, too, contributed to his growing awareness. The Pilgrimages to Jerusalem for festivals like Passover were not frequent, but they were immersive. Imagine the city crowded with pilgrims, the Temple glowing with incense smoke, the Levites singing psalms with measured precision. Imagine walking among strangers, seeing Roman soldiers casually inspecting the crowds, hearing the murmurs of merchants, and witnessing the tension between devotion and authority. Each visit offered a microcosm of the wider world, ritual, law, culture, and politics all in one bustling, overwhelming cityscape.

And then there was the sense of waiting. This wasn't just the anticipation that comes from adolescence or education. It was something more, woven into centuries of Jewish expectation. The people around him whispered of a coming Messiah, each prophecy and hope layering upon the last. The exiles, the returnees, the teachers, they all spoke in echoes of longing. It was in the air, like pollen, and Jesus breathed it in with every step.

It was also a time of inner reflection. Alone, in the hills, by the streams, in the quiet of the night, he must have wondered about purpose. He would have seen the inequities of the world, the suffering of the poor, the compromises of the powerful, and the small, unheralded acts of goodness that often went unnoticed. He observed human nature in its full spectrum from kindness to cruelty, devotion to indifference, humility to arrogance. In this observation, he began to cultivate a vision, not of personal glory, but of understanding, compassion, and direction.

Family and community life reinforced these lessons. Interactions with parents, siblings, and neighbours taught patience, empathy, and leadership. Arguments, reconciliations, celebrations, and funerals, became the fabric through which he learned about human hearts, relationships, and the moral universe. Each day, each laborious task, each quiet observation was a rehearsal for something far larger.

And so he waited. Not in idleness, not in fear, not in simple passivity, but in a conscious preparation. He lived fully attentive to the lessons hidden in work, study, prayer, and observation. He sharpened discernment, cultivated compassion, and deepened his understanding of the spiritual and social world around him.

This quiet period, largely invisible to history, was essential. It was the time in which the observer became a thinker, and in which a boy from a modest Galilean town came to understand himself as part of a story far larger than any village, any Temple, or any generation. The stage was being set. The threads of history, prophecy, law, and human experience were being woven into a tapestry that would soon begin to unfold in public life, with ripples that would stretch across centuries.

And then, just over the horizon of history, there emerged a voice crying out in the wilderness, a herald who would mark the transition from private preparation to public mission, from expectation to action.

Chapter Twenty Six - John the Baptist

In the remote wilderness of Judea, a man appeared whose very presence seemed to crackle with significance. John, the Baptist.

John was an unusual figure by any standard. He did not dwell in towns or villages, did not wear fine clothes, and did not cultivate a life of comfort. Instead, he lived in the desert, among the dry stones, scrubby bushes, and wandering animals. Locusts were his occasional meal and honey from wild bees his only sweetener. He wore garments made of camel hair, a rough, scratchy attire that probably made daily movement uncomfortable, but which marked him as a prophet, a man out of place in society, intentionally so.

People came from Jerusalem, Judea, and the surrounding regions. They walked miles over dusty roads, over hills and across river crossings, drawn by reports of a man proclaiming repentance and preparing the way. Caravans of people trudging through the wilderness, children complaining, elders huffing, all of them compelled by curiosity, devotion, or sheer fear of divine expectation. They came to confess, to be baptised, to hear his strange, passionate proclamations.

John spoke of repentance, not as a casual apology, but as a profound reorientation of life. His words carried the weight of law, prophecy, and moral urgency. He was calling the people to change, to re-align themselves with God's covenant, to live consciously as part of a story stretching back to Abraham and forward to something not yet revealed. His voice, amplified by the open expanse of desert and sky, had a clarity and intensity that could make the mundane world feel charged with sacred possibility.

And then, there was Jesus. It is worth pausing to imagine the quiet anticipation, the subtle tension in a young man who had spent decades learning, observing, reflecting, and preparing. He had lived in Nazareth, worked as a carpenter, studied the Torah, participated in festivals, absorbed the stories of his people, and walked the roads and hills of Galilee. Every experience had shaped him, but now something was stirring. It was a transition from preparation to purpose, from private awareness to public engagement.

When Jesus came to John in the wilderness, the moment was understated but monumental. The baptism was simple, a ritual immersion in the Jordan River, water washing over body and spirit, symbolising repentance, renewal, and readiness. The heavens were described as opening, a spirit descending, a voice affirming what had long been anticipated. It was a confirmation, that the stage had been set for the unfolding of events that would soon ripple across Judea and beyond.

The crowd watched, murmured, and wondered. Some probably did not fully understand what had happened.

Jesus now stepped into the public sphere, conscious that his life was entering a new phase.

The wilderness itself seemed to mark the transition. It was stark, unadorned, challenging, and pure. It was an environment where distractions were stripped away, where human concerns were reduced to essentials, and where clarity of purpose could emerge. John, living fully in that wilderness, became the threshold. The one who prepared the way, the voice that cried in the desert, the figure that bridged expectation and action.

And so, Jesus moved from the quiet life of Nazareth to the open, often harsh, yet profoundly symbolic spaces of public calling. He was no longer just a boy or young man learning the rhythms of life. He was entering a stage where his presence, his identity, and his purpose would begin to intersect with history in ways visible to others. The world of labour, familial care, and synagogue study had prepared him for this moment. The voice of prophecy, the lessons of law, and the anticipation of centuries, all of it converged in the Jordan River, in the wilderness, and in the subtle yet unmistakable awakening of public mission.

Chapter Twenty Seven – Teachings of Jesus

After his baptism and the affirmation from above, Jesus did not immediately perform dramatic miracles or deliver sweeping sermons. Rather, he began quietly, deliberately, moving among the people, observing, listening, and learning the patterns of public life from the perspective of someone already conscious of his purpose. The Galilean towns and villages, with their winding lanes, stone houses, and bustling markets, became the stage on which his ministry would unfold.

In Capernaum people carried baskets of produce along narrow streets, children ran barefoot across sun-baked stones, women drew water from communal wells, and men haggled over prices or laboured in workshops. Roman soldiers made occasional appearances, reminding citizens of distant imperial authority, while local leaders and elders monitored affairs of synagogue, taxation, and communal order. Into this everyday scene stepped Jesus, young but deliberate, observant but unassuming.

He began by visiting synagogues, not as an outsider, but as someone steeped in the Torah, confident in the rhythms of worship and the texts that guided life. His presence drew curiosity. People noticed him because of his deep understanding of scripture and the way he seemed to engage not just with words, but with thought itself. Conversations were different when he spoke, not loud, not ostentatious, but attentive, precise, and deeply reflective.

At first, his actions were small, subtle gestures of compassion, helping the sick, speaking to those ignored by society, breaking social barriers by engaging with women, tax collectors, and others on the margins. People noticed the combination of empathy, insight, and authority. Whispers began: "Who is this man? Where does he come from?"

Movement through the towns and villages was not glamorous. Travel was dusty, hot, and slow. Roads were uneven, rivers had to be crossed, and the weather could be punishing. Yet every journey provided opportunities for observation, reflection, and interaction. Jesus walked among farmers, fishermen, merchants, and families, learning the practical rhythms of daily life, the struggles of people, and the ways in which faith intersected with need.

The wilderness experiences of his youth, the quiet reflection, the immersion in scripture, and the contemplation of human nature were now applied in public life. He noticed hypocrisy and injustice, yes, but also courage, ingenuity, and kindness. He saw how religious leaders sometimes enforced law without compassion, and how the marginalized navigated a world that often overlooked them. These observations would inform every word, gesture, and decision in the early days of his ministry.

Small crowds began to follow him, drawn by reputation, curiosity, or the sense that something unusual had entered their world. Some came hoping for miracles, others for teaching, and some simply for reassurance or solace. Jesus moved among them as a human being fully aware of his purpose but not yet performing the iconic acts that would later define him. He listened, questioned, comforted, and instructed. People felt seen, which was often enough to make a moment unforgettable.

The political backdrop was never far from view. Roman authorities maintained control, Jewish leaders enforced law, and local customs carried weight. Life was structured yet tense, filled with expectation, resistance, and routine. Jesus navigated these realities carefully. He understood that change was not only spiritual but social, and that his actions and words would ripple outward slowly, in ways both subtle and profound.

People spoke of him with wonder, noting not just what he did but the clarity and authority with which he did it. Even without parables, even before the full revelation of his teaching, there was a sense that history, expectation, and divine purpose were intersecting in a tangible way.

The early ministry of Jesus, then, was a delicate balance of moving among people, observing, understanding, and quietly asserting presence while interacting with daily life, politics, and religion. Gradually he was revealing a character, purpose, and authority that would soon expand beyond any one village or town. It was a public awakening grounded in human experience, social observation, and spiritual insight and a beginning that was modest yet unmistakably profound.

As the days and months passed, word of Jesus' presence began to travel beyond the dusty lanes of Galilean villages. People came from towns and countryside alike, bringing curiosity, hope, scepticism, or sometimes just a desire for a moment of attention in a world that often ignored them. Merchants pausing their work to see him speak, women carrying children on their hips, elders leaning on walking sticks, and young men gathering in small clusters, whispering theories about who he was. Each had their own reasons for coming, yet all contributed to a sense of mounting anticipation.

Jesus moved among them without fanfare. He spoke quietly but with unmistakable authority, engaging with individuals, answering questions, and often asking questions in return. He listened carefully, as though he were cataloguing human experience in real time, weighing each concern, each fear, and each hope. People noticed that he seemed to understand more than they said that he could see beneath appearances that he spoke in ways that cut to the heart of the matter. It was subtle, yet profoundly compelling.

The attention he drew did not go unnoticed by the religious leaders. Priests, scribes, and Pharisees were trained in law, debate, and ritual. They understood the power of influence and reputation. They observed quietly at first, noting how crowds seemed unusually attentive, how conversations became charged with meaning. Some were curious, some apprehensive, and some deeply uneasy. There was an invisible tension growing, a sense that the patterns of village and synagogue life were beginning to shift.

Meanwhile, his earliest followers were drawn not just by wonder, but by recognition. They saw in him a combination of knowledge, empathy, moral clarity, and quiet authority. They observed the way he treated people, neighbours, strangers, marginalized folk, and even the critics, with a presence that seemed to demand respect without demanding submission. These followers were fishermen accustomed to toil, tax collectors wary of authority, women who often existed on the edges of public life. Yet in him, they found direction, insight, and a sense of purpose that transcended their daily routines.

Daily life continued around him, even as attention grew. The markets, the olive groves, the narrow streets of towns, and the hillsides of Galilee maintained their rhythms, but now they were punctuated by pauses of people stopping to watch, to hear, and to reflect. Jesus moved with awareness. It was a dance between expectation, social reality, and divine purpose, one that required patience, observation, and subtlety.

The wilderness echoes of his early life still informed his public conduct. He was attentive to nature, to human emotion, to the nuances of power and vulnerability. He understood the limitations of human authority, the tension between law and compassion, and the quiet dignity of labour. Each conversation, each encounter, each step through a village or across a hillside became part of a larger tapestry.

The narrative was slowly unfolding with the shaping of perception, the subtle alignment of followers, the careful observation of opposition, and the steady increase of public presence. The world was taking notice, though not fully aware of what it was seeing.

In short, these early days of public life were a study in subtlety and observation. Jesus moved among people, attended to their needs, understood their fears, and cultivated the authority and presence that would soon define his ministry.

Chapter Twenty Eight - The kingdom revealed in parables

After months of quiet preparation, observation, and subtle public engagement, the moment came for Jesus to begin revealing not just who he was, but the nature of the Kingdom he had come to proclaim. The crowds that had been drawn by curiosity, conversation, and rumour now had something tangible to encounter.

It began with parables, simple stories crafted from everyday life but charged with moral and spiritual significance. Imagine Jesus sitting by the lakeside, the sun warming the stones, children playing nearby, fishermen untangling nets, women carrying water home. He spoke of seeds falling on different soil, of lost sheep and prodigal sons, of treasures hidden in fields, and of lights placed not under a bowl but on a stand to shine for all to see. Each story was drawn from experience, the kind of thing people might see every day and yet each carried layers of insight about justice, mercy, compassion, and God's care.

The parables were subtle but profound. They challenged assumptions, asked listeners to see the world differently, and revealed the contours of a Kingdom unlike any earthly realm. People leaned in, listening closely, thinking deeply, discussing and debating long after he had moved on. And the beauty of these stories was that they could be understood on many levels, even simple enough for a child to grasp, yet rich enough for scholars to wrestle with for a lifetime.

Alongside these stories came acts that defied understanding. Miracles were not mere displays of power. They were signs, gestures that revealed the character of the Kingdom itself. Blind eyes were opened, lame legs strengthened, lepers healed, storms calmed, and bread multiplied. These acts astonished crowds, not simply for the spectacle, but because they revealed a world reordered, where suffering could be relieved, hope restored, and God's presence made tangible.

Each miracle was embedded in daily life. A child healed in a dusty village lane, a storm stilled while fishermen worked their nets, a feast stretched to feed hungry families, these were not abstract wonders. The miracles were invitations to see the world differently, to imagine a life aligned with God's will.

Yet this growing influence did not go unnoticed by authorities. Religious leaders grew concerned. The parables challenged entrenched interpretations of law, questioned rigid rituals, and highlighted mercy over strict adherence. Roman authorities, though initially observing from a distance, began to recognize the potential for social unrest. The combination of popular following, moral authority, and subtle challenge to established norms made the movement impossible to ignore.

Meanwhile, followers multiplied. People all recognized in Jesus someone who combined understanding, compassion, and authority. They were drawn not only to his words and actions, but to the way he made them feel seen, understood, and invited into a larger story. Discipleship became a lived experience, following him through villages, helping him, listening, and witnessing first-hand the Kingdom in motion.

The Kingdom revealed in parables and miracles was not a distant, abstract concept. It was immediate, visible, and participatory. It challenged assumptions, disrupted expectations, and invited people into a new understanding of life, God, and human responsibility. And yet, it remained deeply rooted in the rhythms of daily life.

In these early days of public teaching and miraculous signs, the narrative arc of Jesus' ministry became unmistakable. He was not simply a teacher, a healer, or a figure of curiosity. He was a living revelation of God's Kingdom, moving deliberately among people, revealing its character through stories and acts, inviting participation, reflection, and transformation. The Kingdom had arrived, quietly but unmistakably, in parables whispered across hillsides and miracles performed.

Picture a small village in Galilee, late afternoon sun slanting over terraced hills, dust swirling along the narrow streets. Children are running in laughter, women are carrying water from the well, and men are returning from fields with the weariness of labour etched into their faces. Into this scene,

Jesus begins to speak, drawing listeners with the subtle authority of someone who has lived among them and knows their hearts.

He tells them a story. There was a man with two sons. The younger son, restless, ambitious and impatient, asks for his inheritance early. Imagine the father's face, a mixture of shock, disbelief, and sorrow, handing over what he had spent years building for his family. It is almost scandalous, a breach of tradition and trust. Still the father handed his son the inheritance.

The younger son leaves the village. He travels to distant towns, spending his wealth on extravagant pleasures like feasts, parties, perhaps fleeting friendships, all of it wrapped in laughter, music, and the careless energy of youth. But as with all reckless indulgence, the pleasure is temporary. The money dwindles, alliances fade, and hunger begins to gnaw, not just at the stomach, but at the spirit. He is left alone, with nothing but regret, surrounded by strangers who do not care for his plight.

In desperation, he reflects on his home, the village, the family, the father who had once trusted him. He remembers the simple meals, the work in the fields, the quiet evenings of shared stories, and strange longing blooms. It is not just hunger for food, but a hunger for belonging, for acceptance, for home. He resolves to return, not with arrogance, not expecting celebration, but hoping for mercy, prepared to be treated as a servant rather than a son.

And then, the moment arrives. He approaches the village, unsure, heart pounding. But the father, seeing him from a distance, does something remarkable. He runs. Not slowly, not cautiously, but runs, an elderly man, perhaps a bit stiff with age, yet propelled by love and longing. He embraces the younger son, kisses him. Then takes him indoors and dresses him not as a servant but as a son, and orders a feast. The story lingers here, love shown, at the reversal of expectations, at the joy that is neither earned nor deserved but freely given.

Meanwhile, the older son, returning from the fields, hears the music, sees the celebration of his brother's return, and feels a pang of indignation. He confronts the father, years of obedience, of toil, and of silent sacrifice, seem to count for nothing in comparison to this sudden forgiveness. The father responds gently, explaining that love and grace are not a ledger to be balanced, but a gift to be extended freely. The elder son is invited to join the celebration, to witness that mercy does not diminish justice but expands it, that love is not finite but generous and abundant.

Jesus' listeners hear this story and recognize themselves in it. Some see the younger son, the one who strays, who falters, and who longs for return. Some see the older son, the one who labours, obeys, and struggles with resentment. Others see the father, love made active, mercy made visible, grace extended without calculation. The parable resonates because it is not a distant abstraction.

The brilliance of the story lies in its simplicity and depth. Family dynamics, work, disappointment, celebration, becomes a canvas for the divine. Human emotions such as fear, shame, longing, resentment, and joy are illuminated, and through them, listeners glimpse the character of God who is patient, generous, forgiving, and always ready to welcome the lost home.

And so, on a Galilean hillside, Jesus tells a story that is timeless. The Parable of the Prodigal Son becomes a lens through which every listener, every generation, can see both themselves and the Kingdom of God and a place where grace, mercy, and love are abundant, even in the midst of human failure.

On another day something miraculous happened, it was late morning in a sun-warmed corner of Galilee. The air was dry but carried the subtle fragrance of olive groves, tilled fields, and the occasional waft of bread baking in stone ovens. A large crowd had gathered, five thousand men, not counting women and children, who had followed Jesus across dusty roads and over rolling hills, drawn by the stories of his teachings, the quiet authority of his presence, and the promise of hope in a world often harsh and unforgiving.

The people had come hungry in more ways than one. Many had walked for hours, and stomachs were growling, spirits, too, were weary from daily toil, taxes, and the small disappointments of life in a land under occupation. As the sun climbed higher, murmurs began: "What will we eat?" The disciples looked around, anxiety flickering in their eyes. The crowd seemed impossibly large. Practicality and common sense suggested there was no way to feed so many.

Jesus, standing quietly at the centre of the gathering, took in the scene. He observed the crowd with a patience cultivated over years of walking among people, listening, and understanding. And then, with a calm that contrasted sharply with the rising anxiety, he asked a question: "Where is the food?" Not in reproach, but in gentle prompting.

A boy stepped forward, shy and hesitant, offering a humble lunch of five small loaves of bread and two fish, packed simply in a basket. It was almost laughable, a pittance compared to the need, but the gesture carried something larger. Jesus took the loaves and fish, lifted his eyes toward the sky, and gave thanks. An acknowledgment that even the smallest provision, when placed in divine hands, could become enough.

The distribution began. The loaves were broken, the fish portioned, and baskets were passed from hand to hand. At first, it seemed impossible, barely enough to satisfy a few dozen. But somehow, it multiplied. People ate until they were full, laughter and murmurs blending with the warm Galilean breeze. Children's eyes widened at the abundance, elders nodded in quiet amazement, and the disciples, who had been sceptical, could only watch in astonishment.

By the time the crowd had eaten their fill, twelve baskets of leftovers were collected, miraculous not only for the sheer quantity, but as a sign of the abundance that comes when need meets generosity, faith, and divine action. The miracle was not just the multiplication of food, it was a vivid lesson in care, provision, and the Kingdom that Jesus was beginning to reveal.

The crowd went home transformed, carrying more than the memory of a full stomach. They carried wonder, awe, and the quiet sense that the world could be different, that care could be abundant. Parents recounted the story to children, neighbours discussed it, and even the disciples began to glimpse the scope of what their teacher had come to do.

In the Galilean hills that day a small boy's lunch, a quiet teacher's blessing, and the shared hunger of thousands converged to reveal something profound. Jesus showed that provision, care, and generosity were not limited by scarcity and that the Kingdom could be experienced in tangible, visible ways.

The feeding of the five thousand became a miracle that people could see, touch, and taste, yet one that carried spiritual resonance far beyond the hills of Galilee. It was a moment where history, humanity, and divine intention intersected, quietly but unmistakably.

Chapter Twenty Nine - Opposition and conflict

As crowds grew around Jesus, so did unease. What had begun as curiosity and wonder now began to ripple into tension, and the rhythms of Galilean life were starting to be disrupted. Villages whispered about him in marketplaces, homes, and synagogue steps. Some people were inspired, others unsettled, and a few deeply disturbed. The disruption was subtle at first, but over time it became increasingly palpable.

The religious authorities, trained in law, tradition, and ritual, were the first to register concern. Scribes, Pharisees, and priests had spent years mastering the interpretation of Torah, ensuring observance, and maintaining social and spiritual order. Jesus' parables, miracles, and growing following posed questions they could not answer with routine formulas. Here was a man who spoke with authority, who interpreted scripture in ways that highlighted mercy over strict rule, and who challenged the comfortable structures of power and piety. Their unease was compounded by the way people responded to him by listening, questioning, and following.

Roman authorities, though more distant, were not oblivious. Judea and Galilee were regions under careful watch. Roman governance relied on order and control. A popular figure, even one ostensibly preaching peace and morality, could become a spark for unrest. Soldiers observed gatherings, governors received reports, and subtle surveillance ensured that potential challenges to imperial control did not go unnoticed. Tension was growing, like the air before a summer storm.

Meanwhile, Jesus' growing circle of followers also began to feel the pressure. Men and women who had been drawn to his teaching, who had witnessed miracles and felt the hope he inspired, now faced questions, scepticism, and sometimes hostility from neighbours, relatives, and local leaders. Loyalty became a quiet test. Following him meant not only admiration and wonder, but also confrontations, ridicule, and risk.

The conflict was both personal and societal. In villages, there were murmurs of resentment: "Why does he speak like this? Who does he think he is?" In synagogues, elders debated how to respond, whether to confront him publicly, attempt subtle discrediting, or monitor and wait. Questions arose about tradition, law, and authority. Was this man speaking truth, or was he dangerous? Could someone claim divine authority without destabilizing the community?

Even Jesus' own approach was measured. He did not seek confrontation for its own sake, nor did he provoke for spectacle. Instead, he continued to teach, heal, and engage with people, aware that tension was inevitable. He understood the delicate balance. To reveal the Kingdom of God in tangible ways while navigating human scepticism, entrenched authority, and social structures that were slow to change.

Conflict manifested in multiple ways. Religious leaders questioned him publicly, challenging interpretation of law, Sabbath observance, and ritual purity. They scrutinized his associates, tested him with pointed questions, and attempted to entrap him with logic, legalism, or cultural expectation. At the same time, citizens argued among themselves, some defended him, some doubted and some worried about the implications of following someone so different from established norms.

Yet, in this tension, miracles continued to inspire wonder, parables continued to illuminate the Kingdom, and the people who observed, listened, and participated began to glimpse a world reordered by mercy, compassion, and divine care. Conflict, in a sense, became part of the narrative. It was the pressure against which the truth of his mission would shine, revealing both human resistance and the persistent call of grace.

The opposition was not only inevitable, it was formative. It clarified the stakes and underscored the profound courage required to challenge entrenched systems while embodying compassion and justice. In every whispered accusation, in every sceptical glance, in every subtle challenge from authority, the path of Jesus' ministry became sharper, more defined, and more historically resonant.

In short, the growing tension was the crucible through which expectation, social order, and divine purpose collided. Jesus moved through it with deliberate awareness, balancing authority with empathy, visibility with humility, and action with reflection.

Chapter Thirty - The Last Supper

Evening fell over Jerusalem with a softness that belied the tension thickening in the city. The streets, once bustling with merchants and pilgrims, were quieter now, lit by flickering lamps and the fading glow of a desert sun. Inside a modest upper room, a simple table had been prepared. The smell of bread, herbs, and roasted lamb mingled with the subtle scent of oil lamps burning low, creating an intimate, almost sacred atmosphere.

Jesus sat at the table with his twelve closest companions. Conversation flowed with familiarity, teasing, questions, concerns, memories of shared journeys. And yet, beneath the surface of companionship, there was a quiet tension, a sense that the night carried weight beyond anything they had yet experienced.

Jesus took bread into his hands, breaking it with a deliberate calm that drew all eyes. He passed it to them, saying that it was his body, given for them. It was a gesture both simple and profound, sustenance transformed into a symbol of deeper connection, sacrifice, and trust. The disciples watched, some with understanding, some puzzled, some sensing that the moment carried a significance they could not yet fully grasp.

He then took a cup, rich with wine, and offered it as a symbol of covenant, of life shared, of forgiveness and promise and said that this was his blood poured out for many. The act was intimate, tangible, immediate, and significant.

The conversation turned toward loyalty, trust, and the challenges ahead.

Jesus spoke, as he had throughout their travels, gently, deliberately, with that quiet authority that seemed to make the world pause. And then he said something that made the air cold: "One of you will betray me."

Peter, always impulsive, leaned forward, his voice a mix of bravado and disbelief. "Surely not I?" he asked, eyes bright with earnestness. Others, quieter, perhaps more observant, looked inward, considering their own hearts and motives. John, sitting nearest Jesus, may have sensed the weight of what was coming but could only watch, silent and attentive.

Judas sat among them, outwardly calm, mask of composure firmly in place. His hands rested on the table, and he nodded when spoken to, yet behind the composed expression a storm of thought raged. The deal had been made with the temple authorities, a contract of betrayal, a crossing of loyalty for payment, a turning from friend to facilitator of what would soon unfold. Rationalizations and excuses fluttered through his mind. He told himself it had to be done and that the moment seemed inevitable.

Judas rose. The room, quiet and intimate, seemed to hold its breath. The disciples' attention followed his movements, curiosity mixed with lingering unease. With each step toward the city streets, Judas carried the weight of his decision, the moral gravity of an act that would fracture trust, fracture hearts, and catalyse events far beyond his imagining.

Chapter Thirty One - Arrest, trial, and crucifixion

After supper, Jesus walked with his disciples, leading them to a place where they could pray and reflect, away from the watchful eyes of the city. Jesus withdrew a little, falling to his knees. Here was a man fully aware of what lay ahead, struggling with fear, sorrow, and anticipation. He prayed in earnest, asking, if it were possible that the coming suffering might be averted. His voice was quiet but resolute, mingling with the rustling of the olive leaves, as if the world itself bore witness to the weight of this prayer.

And then Judas arrived. The shadows shifted as he approached with a small cohort of temple guards and officials, lanterns flickering, faces partially hidden, weapons glinting in the night. Judas walked directly to Jesus, the weight of choice and treachery pressing down upon him. He greeted him with a kiss, a gesture that, in any other context, would have signified affection and friendship. But here, it became a signal of betrayal, an intimate act transformed into treachery.

"Greetings" Judas said, his voice calm, controlled, masking the inner storm of conscience, fear, and rationalization. The soldiers immediately recognized Jesus and moved to seize him.

Chaos erupted. The disciples, caught off guard, reacted instinctively. Peter, impulsive and protective, drew a sword and struck, cutting off the ear of one of the guards. Jesus, however, rebuked the violence, touching the moment with calm authority. No resistance, no retaliation, only acceptance of the path that had been foretold. He healed the injured man, underscoring once again the Kingdom he had come to reveal.

Judas' act had succeeded. The man he had walked with shared bread and teaching with, was now in the hands of the authorities. The disciples were stunned, fearful, and uncertain. Confusion and sorrow mingled with adrenaline, the reality of betrayal settling across their hearts.

Jesus was led away quietly, avoiding public uproar but not the gravity of history. Judas followed, a small figure amidst soldiers, walking the path of weakness and moral failure, carrying with him the consequences of choice, conscience, and greed. The disciples, now left in the garden, wrestled with grief, fear, and disbelief, trying to reconcile loyalty with the betrayal they had just witnessed.

The Garden of Gethsemane, in that hour, became a crucible of emotion.

Inside the high priest's residence, the air was thick with heated murmurs. The council of religious leaders, the Sanhedrin, had convened hurriedly, their robes brushing against polished stone floors, their voices a mixture of authority, expectation, and uncertainty. Here was a man who had drawn crowds, challenged long-held interpretations of the Law, and unsettled social and religious hierarchies. They needed a verdict, a way to assert control, but the path was far from simple.

Jesus stood quietly, composed but alert. The accusations were many including claims of blasphemy, of challenging God, of threatening the social and religious order. Witnesses were called, some truthful, some clearly invented. The tension was almost theatrical. Each word, gesture, and pause carried weight.

Peter, meanwhile, struggled with fear and confusion. He had followed at a distance, hiding in shadows, and when questioned about knowing Jesus, he denied it, not once, but three times, in moments that would later echo with sorrow and remorse. The instinct for self-preservation clashed violently with loyalty, revealing the complexities of faith under pressure.

By dawn, the council had made its decision. Jesus would be handed over to the Roman authorities. The religious leaders lacked the legal authority to execute, and political stability mattered more than justice in their eyes. They needed the governor to act.

Jesus was then taken to Pontius Pilate, the Roman governor, who sat in the judgment seat, draped in the trappings of imperial authority. The contrast could not have been greater, a small, calm figure accused of subversion, standing before the apparatus of empire, a room filled with guards, attendants, and officials accustomed to control and obedience.

The questioning was sharp, procedural, and tinged with tension. Pilate asked the simple, direct question: "Are you the King of the Jews?" The answer was quiet, measured, and profound, neither evasive nor inflammatory. Jesus did not deny it, nor did he proclaim it in the way the political authorities expected. Pilate, sensing no immediate threat, yet under pressure from the crowd and the temple authorities, hesitated. He sought to release Jesus, offering a choice to the people between Jesus and another prisoner named Barabbas. This release was a custom during the feast. But the crowd, stirred by leaders and fear, demanded Jesus' execution and the release of Barabbas, who was a man described as a rebel and murderer.

Judas' betrayal had set this chain in motion, Peter's fear had exposed human frailty, and the authorities' need for control had sealed the fate. Pilate washed his hands in a symbolic gesture, declaring that he was innocent of the blood, yet had yielded to the pressure.

Throughout, Jesus remained composed, embodying both patience and vulnerability. His silence, calm responses, and dignity highlighted the contrast between the petty ambitions, fear, and malice of the men judging him and the transcendence of his purpose.

By mid-morning, the verdict was final. Jesus was sentenced to be crucified, the culmination of betrayal, human weakness, fear, political calculation, and divine purpose converging in a single city street now heavy with consequence.

The trials revealed not only the human dynamics of fear, loyalty, ambition, and authority but also the resilience and moral clarity of one man confronting the forces arrayed against him. The whispered accusations, the flawed testimony, the crowd's cries created a moment that would echo through centuries.

The streets of Jerusalem were narrow, uneven, and crowded, even in the early morning. A restless city waking to the knowledge of what was about to unfold. Into this chaos, a procession moved, slow and deliberate.

Jesus, already bruised and exhausted from the night of trials, the false accusations, and the scourging, was led through the streets. The soldiers forced him to carry the wooden beam that would become part of the cross, a heavy, awkward burden that scraped his shoulders and made each step an exercise in endurance and human suffering. Every cobblestone pressed into flesh, every stumble a reminder of fragility and mortality.

Crowds lined the streets. Some wept quietly, recognizing the injustice, while others jeered, caught up in anger, fear, or manipulation.

At one point, Jesus faltered under the weight, his body wracked with fatigue and pain. The soldiers, seeing the slowing of the procession, pressed a passer-by, Simon of Cyrene, into service to carry the cross. A reluctant helper, Simon's life collided with circumstance. This simple act of assistance now part of history's largest stage of human suffering.

As they reached Golgotha, the hill outside the city walls, the scene became more surreal. The sky, already pale with the morning sun, seemed heavier, as if the world itself was aware of the significance. Soldiers prepared the instruments of execution.

Jesus was laid upon the cross. Nails pierced his flesh and the wood pressed unyieldingly against his skin and bone. The crowd watched, some horrified, some indifferent, some moved beyond words. The city, with its streets, markets, and walls, now framed a moment that would echo across millennia.

Above the hill, the sky darkened unusually, a phenomenon that seemed to pause time. Jesus spoke, offering words of forgiveness and comfort even in pain, to the criminals beside him, to the people, to the disciples, to humanity itself.

Hours passed slowly. Then finally, as Jesus' took his final breath, witnesses recoiled.

The body was taken down and laid in a tomb, a simple cave carved from rock, and unadorned. The streets emptied slowly, leaving behind stones, shadows, and the memory of an event that would define history, faith, and imagination for generations.

Chapter Thirty Two - Resurrection of Jesus

The streets of Jerusalem, now quieter after the tumult of the crucifixion, carried the heavy scent of sweat, blood, and dust. A hush lingered, as if the city itself sensed the weight of what had just passed.

Joseph of Arimathea, a wealthy and respected man, moved quietly but decisively. With courage and care, he approached Pilate to request the body of Jesus, an act of respect layered with significance. Pilate perhaps wearied by the day's events or recognizing no threat in the act, granted the request.

The body, now lifeless, was handled with tenderness and ritual. Nicodemus brought a mixture of myrrh and aloes, fragrant and earthy, intended to honour the dead and slow the decay of flesh. Together, they wrapped Jesus in linen, each fold deliberate, each gesture a quiet testament of loyalty, compassion, and grief.

The tomb itself was a cave carved from rock, hewn into the hillside. A large stone was rolled across the entrance, sealing the body within, creating both a barrier and a sanctuary. Soldiers were stationed to watch, an extra measure meant to prevent theft, but also a reminder of human suspicion, authority, and fear.

The disciples and followers left the scene in a mixture of grief, confusion, and awe. Mary Magdalene, Mary the mother of Jesus, and others lingered, carrying a quiet weight of sorrow, their hearts heavy with love, despair, and the echo of the events that had unfolded.

The days that followed were slow, each moment stretched by uncertainty. The Sabbath arrived, demanding rest, reflection, and the suspension of work. The disciples hid, weary and fearful, wrestling with questions, and doubts.

And then, in the quiet predawn hours of the third day, something unexpected occurred. The stone, once heavy and immovable, had been rolled away. The tomb, sealed and guarded, now lay open. Mary Magdalene and others approached, carrying spices, their routine pilgrimage of devotion interrupted by awe and confusion. Inside, the body was gone.

And then Jesus appeared. Not as a ghost or a shadow, but alive, tangible, speaking, present. To Mary, he first appeared in the garden, asking her simply, "Why are you crying?" Her grief and devotion collided with astonishment and recognition, and in that moment, fear gave way to the first, tentative joy of resurrection.

Over the following days, Jesus appeared repeatedly to the disciples. In closed rooms where fear had driven them to hide, he entered unbidden, a quiet yet unmistakable presence. Hands once nailed and now healed and feet, once bruised and now strong. Eyes meeting theirs with a combination of reassurance, challenge, and gentle authority. Each encounter was intimate, human, and yet charged with divine significance.

Thomas, initially sceptical, touched the wounds, felt the truth in the flesh, and finally moved from doubt to belief. Each disciple wrestled with emotions of relief, wonder, reverence, and the dawning understanding that their lives, and indeed the world itself had been irreversibly changed.

The appearances were not mere spectacle. They carried purpose of teaching, reassurance, and commissioning. Jesus reminded them of the path they would follow, the mission they would embrace, and the enduring presence of the Kingdom. It was their turn to continue the work Jesus began, and he gave them the guidance, purpose, and authority to do it.

On a hill outside the city, in a final moment witnessed by the disciples, Jesus ascended, leaving behind the physical presence that had so defined their journey. Yet he did not vanish into abstraction, the disciples experienced both absence and profound presence, the spiritual and moral continuity of the teacher, friend, and guide they had followed. The message was clear. The story continued and the Kingdom endured. Human lives were forever called to witness, act, and believe.

The resurrection transformed fear into courage, grief into hope, and followers into a community imbued with purpose. Their understanding of life, death, and morality shifted, as did their comprehension of loyalty, love, and divine action. The world remained materially the same but perception, faith, and human possibility had been expanded beyond measure.

In the quiet aftermath, the disciples began to move outward, carrying with them the weight of memory, the spark of encounter, and the story that had started in a humble stable, passed through deserts, cities, and hills, endured betrayal, suffering, death, and culminated in resurrection. Hearts had been touched, and through them, the story would ripple outward to generations yet to come.

Chapter Thirty Three - The Pentecost

Imagine a small house in Jerusalem. Not fancy, with stone walls, a few rugs, and maybe a courtyard. Inside, a group of men and women huddled together, wide-eyed, tense, and thoroughly bewildered. They were here for several reasons.

First, fear. The crucifixion had left them rattled. Jesus, their teacher, friend, and guide, had been executed in a spectacle of violence, and if the authorities had their way, who was to say what might happen to them next? The city outside continued its usual bustle with merchants shouting, donkeys braying, children running about, but inside this small room, every shadow and creak seemed loaded with threat. Being together was a natural response. Safety in numbers, reassurance in shared presence.

Second, hope. Jesus had promised that something was coming, though they weren't entirely sure what it would look like. They gathered to pray, to reflect, and to wait. They needed each other to process the bewildering mix of grief, awe, and anticipation.

The third reason was connection. They were all bound by shared history, shared meals, shared fear, and shared purpose. They had walked with Jesus, listened to his teachings, witnessed miracles, and experienced the resurrection.

And then it happened. A sound, like a sudden rush of wind, filled the room. Not a gentle breeze, this was the sort of noise that makes you flinch, perk up, and wonder if a roof is about to collapse.

Languages that nobody in the room had learned flowed effortlessly and loudly from their lips. Greek, Aramaic, Latin, words and phrases that allowed them to speak across cultures, across boundaries, in ways no one could have imagined. It was chaos and clarity all at once.

Outside, a crowd gathered, drawn by the noise and now there was confusion, amazement, and disbelief all rolled together. People were murmuring to one another: "Aren't those Galileans?" they said. "How can we possibly understand them? Each of us hears them in our own language!" It was a bizarre, delightful, head-scratching moment, like hearing a concert you can't quite locate the instruments for, yet understanding every word.

Peter, always the spokesman even when he hadn't planned to be, realized what was happening and saw the opportunity. His fear faded and his courage surged. With a voice that must have trembled slightly but carried with clarity, he addressed the crowd. Words delivered with conviction. He explained that this was the fulfilment of prophecy and that God's Spirit had been poured out. The events that had happened, the crucifixion, and the resurrection were all part of a plan now coming to light.

The crowd reacted in mixed ways. Some scoffed, some laughed, and some were genuinely terrified. Others were moved to awe, their hearts opening to the possibility that what they were witnessing was real, unprecedented, and divine.

And then something happened, Peter and the others urged the listeners to respond, to accept the message, to embrace what God was doing through this fallible, yet Spirit-filled group. In the days that followed, people were baptized, hearts were changed, and a community began to form, not in some grand cathedral but in homes, courtyards, and streets. People, inspired and empowered, were now the agents of these events.

From that moment, the early Christian movement shifted gears. They were now bold, visible, and purposeful, speaking to the city, caring for the poor, healing the sick, and spreading their message far beyond the walls of Jerusalem.

Chapter Thirty Four - Paul's conversion and mission

The disciples are now an even more energetic, audacious group doing things. They speak in languages they never studied, their courage inflamed, and their joy palpable. They step out into the streets, people who now command attention, not because of status or military power, but because their conviction is visible, infectious, and unshakable.

They start preaching, teaching, baptizing. People stop, lean on carts, adjust their robes, and listen. Some are moved and decide to join in. Houses begin filling with prayer, discussion, and food shared in fellowship. Imagine the chaos, discussions spilling into courtyards, children laughing, neighbours peering curiously over walls. And yet, amidst this bustle, something is taking shape, a movement with heart, purpose, and momentum.

And now enter Saul, the man who would become Paul. Up until this point, he is the embodiment of religious zeal gone wrong, a Pharisee with a laser-like focus on persecuting the followers of Jesus. He's determined, fierce, and utterly convinced that he is on the "right" side. He arrests, he interrogates, he intimidates. He's terrifying, at least to anyone who doesn't want trouble.

Then on the road to Damascus, there is a moment that changes everything. Saul is traveling. Probably thinking about his next raid on the fledgling Christian community, when a light brighter than anything he's ever seen knocks him to the ground. And then a voice, unmistakable and commanding, asks, "Saul, Saul, why are you persecuting me?" Saul is blinded, shaken, and probably a little panicked. He is forced to pause, quite literally, and confront the reality of what he has been doing.

Meanwhile God speaks directly to Ananias (a disciple in Damascus) in a vision. God tells him to go to Saul, find him, lay hands on him, and restore his sight. So he goes. He lays hands on Saul, and Saul's sight is restored, and he is baptized. The man who was once the most formidable persecutor becomes one of the most formidable advocates.

"Saul" was his Hebrew name, the one he carried as a Jew from Tarsus, a Pharisee educated in Jewish law, deeply devoted to his religious traditions, and zealous for the Jewish faith. As Saul, he had been focused on preserving Judaism as he understood it, even to the point of persecuting early followers of Jesus.

After his dramatic conversion on the road to Damascus, he was given a new purpose, to take the message of Jesus, not just to Jewish communities, but to the Gentile (non-Jewish) world. "Paul" is his Roman name, the one that would be more accessible and recognizable to the broader Greco-

Roman society. By using this name, he could move more easily through cities across the Roman Empire and engage with diverse communities.

Saul, who was now known as Paul, begins to travel, write, and teach. He boards boats, walks dusty roads, and debates in marketplaces. Merchants, housewives, tentmakers, and fishermen, are now meeting a man whose zeal is reoriented from persecution to preaching, and who combines sharp intellect with raw human passion. He writes letters, careful, thoughtful, sometimes exasperated, and often encouraging. You can almost hear him sigh: "Dear Corinthians, seriously, stop arguing about which spiritual gift is better, rather focus on love." The advice becomes foundational for generations of believers.

Meanwhile, the Christian community continues to grow, quietly and chaotically. People meet in homes, along rivers, wherever they can gather. Meals are shared. Debates occur. People get sick, get married, argue about logistics, and occasionally fall asleep during long prayers. Life is now infused with purpose and guided by the Spirit. Every act is now invested with meaning, whether feeding the hungry, comforting the weak, or explaining a story that, until recently, seemed impossible.

And so, through Pentecost, Peter, Paul, and countless others are thrust into circumstances that transform the initial spark into a movement. Streets, marketplaces, homes, and hillsides become stages for teaching, healing, and fellowship.

Chapter Thirty Five - The growth of the early church

The first Christians, barely fifty or a hundred strong huddled in homes, and small meeting places, talking, praying, and sharing meals. Not particularly impressive in size, certainly not in power or wealth, and yet something remarkable is happening. They are growing. Slowly, unevenly, unpredictably, but undeniably, the movement is spreading.

People join for all sorts of reasons. Some are inspired by the preaching of Peter, James, or Paul. Some are drawn by the sense of community, the warmth of shared meals, and the promise of hope. Others are simply curious, the kind of curiosity that makes you peek into a house where a group of people seems unusually joyful despite the chaos of Roman-occupied Jerusalem.

The growth isn't orderly. It's chaotic and often confusing, but that's exactly the point. This type of growth happens in unexpected ways, not like a spreadsheet neatly ticking off numbers.

Paul and other missionaries travel tirelessly. Boats across the Mediterranean, dusty roads, crowded city square, everywhere, they preach, teach, debate, and write letters. Communities emerge in Corinth, Ephesus, Philippi, Thessalonica, Antioch, and countless other towns. And here's the fascinating part. These communities are built not on coercion or politics but on connection, shared meals, acts of kindness, caring for the sick, supporting widows, resolving disputes, and celebrating together.

Conflict and challenge are constant companions. Persecution, misunderstandings, doctrinal disagreements, and the occasional internal squabble. Imagine trying to keep a growing, dispersed community on the same page without the luxury of phones, email, or instant messaging. People misunderstand letters, arguments break out, yet somehow, the communities endure and expand.

Miracles and unexpected events also accompany growth, not as spectacles for amusement but become proof to believers and a spark for awe in outsiders, healings, deliverances, conversions. The most profound "miracle" is the sheer persistence of people to live, love, and teach according to what they believe, even under threat, uncertainty, and hardship.

So the early church grows, not with grandiose plans or vast armies, but with everyday people navigating the task of embodying faith in real everyday life. Slowly, the movement spreads beyond Jerusalem, across Judea, Samaria, and eventually the Roman Empire.

Chapter Thirty Six - Revelation of hope and new creation

As the early church grew, it became clear that its mission was not merely about preserving what had been taught or performing incredible deeds. At its heart was a message of hope, a vision that promised renewal, and restoration.

The followers of Jesus were convinced that through his life, death, and resurrection, a new reality had been inaugurated. It was a world in which people could find dignity, purpose, and a sense of belonging. It was a vision in which injustices could be addressed, wounds could be healed, and broken relationships restored. This was not abstract theology for ivory towers, it was meant to shape daily life, to guide behaviour, and to offer a way forward in a world that was often harsh, unfair, and unpredictable.

The letters, teachings, and miracles of the early church all pointed to this new creation. Paul, in particular, emphasized that faith in Christ was transformative, not just spiritually but in the very way one lived, traits like patience, kindness, generosity, courage, and love were all signs of this new creation at work. Communities began to function differently. People shared resources, cared for the vulnerable, and supported one another in ways that were startling to outsiders. Life began to reflect hope.

The idea of a "new creation" carried significance. On the one hand, it pointed to the renewal of all things, a promise that the brokenness of the world, including sickness, injustice, and death, would ultimately be set right. On the other, it addressed the human experience here and now, every act of compassion, every reconciled relationship, every courageous step of faith was a participation in the unfolding reality of God's new creation.

Hope, in this sense, was not passive. It was active, demanding engagement with the world using creativity, perseverance, and moral courage. People were invited to become agents of this new creation, to heal, to teach, to care, and to inspire. Each small act of love or justice was a visible sign of the invisible transformation promised by God.

And it was contagious. People saw the hope reflected in the lives of believers and were drawn to it. Miracles could awe, but hope inspired. It gave direction, resilience, and meaning. Communities began to think differently about what life could be, and in the midst of suffering, loss, and uncertainty, they found the promise of renewal.

In essence, the early Christian movement was as much about revealing a vision of what could be as it was about recounting what had been. A new creation already present but not yet fully realized began to emerge. It was both a profound spiritual truth and a practical guide for living, inviting every believer into the work of hope, restoration, and transformation.

Chapter Thirty Seven - The new heaven and new earth

The story starts with creation, the heavens, the earth, the seas, and all their astonishing variety and it ends with another creation, a re-creation. This is not a return to Eden exactly, though the echoes are unmistakable, but rather the fulfilment of what Eden hinted at. A world in which harmony is complete, peace is secure, and God's presence is unbroken. It is called the new heaven and new earth.

John of Patmos. Known simply as "John," was a servant and witness of Jesus, who was exiled to the rocky island of Patmos in the Aegean Sea, likely by Roman authorities. There, in isolation, he received and recorded the visions that became the final book of the Bible.

Now, here's where it gets interesting. For centuries, many Christians assumed this John was the same as John the Apostle, one of the Twelve disciples of Jesus, the brother of James, and the "beloved disciple" mentioned in the Gospel of John. This connection gave the book considerable authority. But modern scholars debate this. The language and style of Revelation are quite different from the Gospel and letters of John, which makes some think it was a different man, also named John, known to the early churches of the large peninsula that makes up most of modern-day Turkey (Asia Minor)

What is clear is that John of Patmos was deeply rooted in the prophetic tradition. His writing echoes the thunder and poetry of Ezekiel, Daniel, and Isaiah, filled with symbolic visions, cosmic imagery, and sharp warnings. He wasn't writing dreamy speculation, but rather a form of resistance literature, messages of hope to persecuted Christians under Roman rule, assuring them that God's justice and renewal would ultimately prevail.

John describes this in vivid, almost unearthly imagery. A city descending like a bride adorned for her husband, streets like polished gold, gates like pearls, light without the need of sun or moon because God himself is present. To the modern reader, it can feel like a kind of dreamscape, heavy with symbolism. But the underlying idea is both simple and profound. The brokenness of the old order, pain, injustice, mourning, and death will be undone.

For the early believers, many of whom lived with persecution, poverty, or grief, the new heaven and new earth were not abstract images of far-off glory, but the assurance that their suffering was not final. Every tear shed, every act of faithfulness offered, every loss endured would be answered by restoration. The story of the world, with all its detours, conflicts, and exiles, would not end in futility but in renewal.

And it is striking how the vision is framed. At the end of the Bible, the separation that marked so much of human experience between heaven and earth, between God and humanity, between hope and reality disappears. Heaven and earth are joined. God dwells among his people. The sacred is no longer distant but part of life. It is a vision not of escape from the world, but of the world transformed, healed, and made whole.

The imagery also brings the story full circle. In Genesis, a garden with rivers gave life to the earth. In Revelation, a river of life flows through the new city, lined with trees whose leaves are for the healing of the nations. The cycle of exile and return that shaped Israel's history finds its final resolution. No more exile, no more scattering, no more distance. Home has at last been restored, but on a scale beyond Eden's simplicity. It is Eden, but expanded, magnified, secured forever.

To read this vision is to be reminded that the Bible's story has always been one of movement, from creation to covenant, from exile to return, from cross to resurrection. The new heaven and new earth are not a sudden departure from the story but its culmination, the point at which every fragment of hope, every promise of renewal, and every glimpse of God's presence is drawn together into a complete and radiant whole.

For the early Christians, this vision wasn't meant to lull them into waiting idly. Quite the opposite, it was a call to live now in the light of what was coming. If God's future was one of healing, justice, and peace, then their present should reflect those realities as much as possible. Each act of kindness, each work of reconciliation, each effort to mend what was broken was a foretaste of that promised world. The new heaven and new earth were both a future to long for and a pattern to live by.

So the Bible ends where it began, with creation, but this time, perfected. Humanity's story, marked so often by frailty and failure, is redeemed. And the invitation remains open to step into the story, to live in its hope.

Epilogue

If there is a single thread that binds the Bible from beginning to end, it is the story of God moving to restore what is broken. From the first breath of creation to the final vision of a new heaven and new earth, the narrative is shaped by a profound truth. Death is not the end, and life is not meaningless. God raises, redeems, and renews. What once seemed irreversible is overcome.

The resurrection of Jesus stands at the centre of this story, a living demonstration that life triumphs over death. It is the proof that God's promise is real. And Revelation's vision of a new heaven and new earth expands that triumph to all creation, a world without pain, without mourning, without final separation and a world where God dwells fully with his people and where the fullness of life is restored.

Yet this story is not only about the distant horizon. It shapes how we live today. The Bible is clear that our choices, faith, and love connect us to that future. Love and compassion, justice and humility, generosity and service, these are not mere ideals. They are the ways in which we participate in God's renewal now. Prayer, worship, and community ground us in the story, reminding us that hope is not passive. Even in the face of suffering, fear, or uncertainty, the faithful are called to live as though God's kingdom is already breaking into the world.

In the grand sweep of scripture, every act of obedience, every gesture of mercy, and every act of faith is part of the larger movement from creation to restoration. The epics of Abraham, Moses, David, Jesus, and the apostles are not distant history alone, they are invitations to join in the ongoing work of redemption.

So the Bible closes with a promise, a new heaven, a new earth, tears wiped away, death conquered, and life renewed. And it invites you to live in alignment with God's character here and now, to embody love, justice, and faithfulness, and to walk with hope in the shadow of resurrection. In this light our struggles are infused with meaning, and the story of God's creation, redemption, and renewal continues through each of us until the ultimate vision is fully realized.

In short, the story of the Bible is a story of hope, renewal, and purpose. And reminds us that the way we live today matters.

Exclusions

Considering that the "Chronicles of the Bible" is intended to capture the sweeping narrative from Genesis through Revelation in a readable flowing style there are naturally a lot of details, minor stories, and specific teachings that are left out for the sake of brevity, clarity, readability, and narrative flow. Here are some of the main things that were left out or lightly touched upon.

1. Genealogies and family lists

- Long genealogical lists in Genesis, Chronicles, and elsewhere (hundreds of names).
- Minor family branches that don't impact the main narrative arc.

2. Detailed laws and rituals

- Levitical codes and priestly regulations.
- Temple rituals, sacrifices, and purity laws.
- Specific ceremonial instructions (e.g. festivals, offerings, cleanliness rules).

3. Repetitive cycles and minor events

- Recurring rebellions during the Judges period.
- Numerous minor battles, territorial skirmishes, and conquests.
- Repeated patterns of sin, punishment, and restoration that are summarized.

4. Complex prophetic visions and symbolic language

- Highly symbolic visions of prophets like Ezekiel and Daniel.
- Localized or time-specific prophecies that don't affect the broader storyline.
- Numbers and symbols being difficult to interpret without context.

5. Apocryphal/deuterocanonical texts

- Books such as Tobit, Judith, Wisdom of Solomon, and Maccabees. Although these texts enrich history and wisdom literature, they are not in all Christian traditions.

6. Detailed letters and early church debates

- Entire text of Paul's letters, with nuanced theological argumentation.
- Minor disputes in early churches and community-specific instructions.

7. Miracles, parables, and encounters

- Every miracle of Jesus and the apostles.
- Lesser-known parables and minor teachings that don't change the overall narrative arc.

8. Political and historical minutiae

- Exact dates, minor kings, political alliances, and boundary changes.
- Localised events that were significant at the time but don't affect the narrative sweep.

9. Individual psalms, proverbs, and wisdom sayings

- Each psalm or proverb is not included, only overarching themes of praise, lament, and wisdom are highlighted.

10. Dark or morally complex stories

- Stories with graphic violence or morally ambiguous elements may be summarized or left out to maintain narrative flow.

Lessons from the Bible

1. **Love matters most.**
   Choose compassion, patience, and kindness, even when it's inconvenient.
2. **Forgive, and be free.**
   Release bitterness and heal relationships.
3. **Stay humble.**
   Humility opens the way to wisdom, empathy, and peace.
4. **Seek justice and show mercy.**
   Care for fairness and act with compassion.
5. **Trust God and don't worry.**
   Focus on today and let God guide the rest.
6. **Keep faith and persevere.**
   Hold on through uncertainty.
7. **Be generous.**
   Giving blesses both the giver and the receiver.
8. **Live honestly and speak with care.**
   Truth and wise words build trust and encouragement.
9. **Be patient.**
   Waiting is trust in God's timing.
10. **Don't give up on people, or yourself.**
    Extend grace as God extends it to you.

11. **Rejoice and be grateful.**
    See life through faith; joy and gratitude turn
    moments into blessings.

12. **Serve others.**
    Humility and selfless action define true greatness.

13. **Seek wisdom.**
    Discern when to act, speak, or stay silent.

14. **Walk in integrity.**
    Let honesty, openness, and goodness guide your
    actions.

15. **Find contentment and courage.**
    Trust God for what you need and stand for what is
    right.

16. **Be still and listen.**
    In silence and reflection, find clarity, peace, and
    God's presence.

www.ingramcontent.com/pod-product-compliance
Lightning Source LLC
Chambersburg PA
CBHW070915130626
46555CB00001B/147